WHEN
THE
PARENTS
CHANGE
EVERYTHING
CHANGES

WHEN THE PARENTS CHANGE

EVERYTHING CHANGES

SEISMIC SHIFTS IN CHILDREN'S BEHAVIOUR

PAUL DIX

Cornerstone Press

1 3 5 7 9 10 8 6 4 2

Cornerstone Press
20 Vauxhall Bridge Road
London SW1V 2SA

Cornerstone Press is part of the Penguin Random House group of companies
whose addresses can be found at global.penguinrandomhouse.com.

Penguin
Random House
UK

First published by Cornerstone Press in 2023

www.penguin.co.uk

A CIP catalogue record for this book is available from the British Library.

ISBN 9781529900132 (hardback)
ISBN 9781529900149 (trade paperback)

Typeset in 12/16pt Dante MT Std by Jouve (UK), Milton Keynes
Printed and bound in Great Britain by Clays Ltd, Elcograf S.p.A.

The authorised representative in the EEA is Penguin Random House Ireland,
Morrison Chambers, 32 Nassau Street, Dublin D02 YH68

www.greenpenguin.co.uk

MIX
Paper | Supporting
responsible forestry
FSC® C018179

Penguin Random House is committed to a
sustainable future for our business, our readers
and our planet. This book is made from Forest
Stewardship Council® certified paper.

To Ellie, Alfie and Bertie, for reminding me that I still have a great deal to learn about my own behaviour.

CONTENTS

INTRODUCTION
CHANGE STARTS AT HOME

Your behaviour is the only behaviour over which you have absolute control. To change your children's behaviour, you first need to change your own.

In the most difficult moments, your behaviour is the difference between chaos and calm. It is the gap between strategies failing or succeeding. It sets the climate for the entire home. Your behaviour is so important that it puts every other factor into a firm second place.

When the Parents Change, Everything Changes is not just a groovy title. It is the central principle you need to save your child's sanity and your own. Without it, nothing else will matter.

That doesn't mean you need to become a different human being overnight. This isn't a magic behaviour solution. But there are deliberate, strategic tweaks you can make in your behaviour towards your child that will in turn transform theirs towards you.

When the parents change, everything changes. That change can start today.

THE BEGINNING

Before I was a parent, I was a teacher. A primary school teacher first, working on short-term contracts in East London. The children were lovely but the schools were under-resourced and struggling. Every Friday I would scour the jobs section in the education press, looking for something more permanent.

Of course, I was a dreamer and enjoyed thinking of what might be if I could escape from the portacabins of 90s Newham and launch myself out into the world. I would start by going straight to jobs that were furthest afield. Every distant land was there: Jamaica, Bermuda, Canada . . . Wigan. Soon, I moved on to the more realistic sections of the classifieds. Until one day I saw a job that looked perfect – if only I was a little more experienced.

It was a head of department role in a secondary school in the West Midlands. I was desperately underqualified. Naturally, I immediately resolved to apply. Fighting through the discouraging cries of my colleagues – 'You aren't qualified for that'; 'It's a job in a secondary school, what do you know about that?' etc. – I fired off my CV.

Seventy-two hours later, the headteacher called me at home. 'You must come to interview!' he said. Basking in the soft glow of his enthusiasm – and of refuting my naysaying colleagues – I got in my car and drove north. Proper north, beyond Harrow, and even the distant lights of Wembley. The job was in a small town near Birmingham. A Londoner born and bred, I had no idea what to expect. But when I arrived in the school car park, it looked innocent enough: pebbledash outhouses, Brutalist concrete – all as *Grange Hill* as you get.

Introduction

I was met in the reception by the headteacher. As he shook my hand warmly, he seemed inexplicably pleased to see me. He told me that the six other candidates had withdrawn from the interview process that morning. 'YES!' I thought. The doors of fate were finally opening. I was ushered briskly into a bare interview room without being shown around the school. They asked me three questions and within ten minutes had offered me the job. I was a head of department. In a secondary school. I didn't have a clue what I was doing.

Feeling the warmth of unexpected triumph, I decided that, before returning to London, I should drive around the estate that the school served; this was my new turf, after all. It was at this point that I realised why the other six candidates had withdrawn. They had had the foresight to take this drive before arriving at the school. And must have driven straight home afterwards. I had landed myself in one of the worst-performing schools in England (11 per cent pass rate at GCSE), on the doorstep of one of the most notorious housing estates in the United Kingdom, in a pocket of raw poverty that ran generations deep.

Two weeks later the school failed an inspection, the head who'd appointed me was unceremoniously sacked, and every excluded student from the special school up the road returned. The chaos ramped up a notch.

My first few weeks were disastrous. I made all the mistakes a young teacher must. I spent long days trying to shout and punish my way to good behaviour, denouncing every mild misdemeanour within 100 yards, enlisting every bull-terrier deputy head I could find, and trying to scare my way to success. It didn't work: 'You're a bit of a prick, aren't you, sir?'

became my life's refrain. And I was. The children couldn't have been less bothered about my penchant for issuing detentions and shouting until the walls shook.

These were children who didn't follow rules. But they did follow people. Some people. There were, I realised, teachers who had what I didn't: respect, borne of proper relationships with the pupils. I needed to learn from them, and quickly.

In the weeks that followed, I began to understand more about the children, their families and their community. Poverty had stripped them of resources, but not their pride, passion and sense of place. These were children who would put you through the ringer for months, before declaring that you were their favourite teacher of all time.

In this school, shouting didn't work. The children were hardened to it. They either simply refused, or accepted it as part of the normal rhythm of their day. What did work was a sense of connection and mutual trust. I learned to meet them where they were, not to try and impose my expectations on them or to treat them as if they had no voice. I told them every day, 'I am not leaving, I care about you, I am here for you,' until they believed me. It didn't work for a few months. And then, suddenly, it did.

It was the worst-behaved children who taught me the most. Those for whom no punishment had any impact, as their home lives were already punishing them enough. I was dealing with children who would tell you to 'fuck off' if you asked them to do something they didn't fancy. Children who would come to school without having washed or eaten in twenty-four hours. Those suffering neglect, witnessing daily domestic abuse and drug addiction. Children who would attack adults, threaten, and swear like a bricky in a flat-roofed boozer. I can play Top Trumps of crazy school stories and win every time.

In those first havoc-filled months I learned as much as the children did. The school taught me how to handle other people's children, often in their worst moments. It taught me how to respond to children who were seemingly out of control, how to get better behaviour by noticing the positive things, how to structure consequences so that they were proportionate and fair. It taught me how to control myself and how to use that self-control to manage the behaviour of others.

It was just one step in a thirty-plus-year career in education – from teaching assistant, to teacher, advisor and trainer – but it changed me as a teacher. Eventually, it would change me as a parent.

CLASSROOM TO PRAM

I remember carrying my first child, Alfie, around the maternity unit, cooing to him gently and promising to be the best parent in the world. Of course, I am not. I am as capable as anyone else of being a great parent one minute and an absolute failure the next. While writing this introduction I have accidentally called my eldest's new girlfriend Charlotte, twice.*

What I do have, however, is a plan and a set of principles which mean that such inconsistencies are ironed out. The

---

* Her name is Emily. The last one was Charlotte.

highs of parenting are still magnificent. But the lows don't feel so low. It is possible to fail better, for your bad days not to affect others, and for your child's bad days not to ruin yours.

My experience in the classroom taught me skills and techniques that were easily transported into the home. The two aren't the same, obviously. But teaching and parenting have more in common than divides them. Particularly when it comes to behaviour.

The most important difference is emotion. When you are telling other people's children what to do and how to behave, there is less emotional connection and guilt. It is easier to stay rational and to not allow personal feelings about the child to cloud your judgement. As a parent, every interaction feels loaded with anxieties about your abilities/your relationship with your child/that time when you shouted really unfairly, etc. I get it. It is tricky to avoid those thoughts.

But this is where a teacher's outlook is most handy. Think back to your favourite teacher at school. Think about how they dealt with behaviour. The best teachers are consistent, fair and calm. In the face of a screaming wall of thirty children – whether six- or sixteen-year-olds – they glide like swans, preventing the wobbliest behaviour, reassuring the most vulnerable, putting out fires without blinking. You know this because you will have been taught by a few. Hopefully more than a few.

Your child is not your pupil. But in dealing with their most difficult behaviours, it can help to draw on the best teachers' practice. Step beyond the emotional confusion of it being your own child, and the principles, skills and techniques that work in the classroom become perfectly transferable to the home.

I know this because I've done it myself. Over the years, I began to develop the tools I'd come up with for changing my own behaviour as a teacher into a method designed to dramatically improve behaviour in schools. I called it 'When the Adults Change, Everything Changes'. To my surprise and delight, this has become a standard method for dealing with the most difficult behaviour in the trickiest schools around the world (as well as in some of the best). It has been tried, tested and celebrated in over 100,000 classrooms. I've talked about the approach in Parliament and worked with the Department of Justice on how it might be used in youth custody, and personally helped thousands of headteachers transform behaviour in their schools.

Over the years I've received hundreds of messages from another group who have used the method to their advantage: parents. They have found that there, too, it works. Not just in theory but in practice. This isn't just a nice story to give you false hope. It changes you. And it changes your child.

So I admit it: the ideas in this book aren't freshly invented. Their foundations lie in decades of teaching your children – or, at least, those who have the same behaviours as yours. I have seen them at their best and walked alongside them at their worst. Being a teacher taught me how to teach behaviour. To your children and to mine.

CALM, CONSISTENT, RELATIONAL PARENTING

The ideas in this book are diverse. But they always come back to a handful of simple, straightforward principles.

Everything starts with your emotions. Focus on the atmosphere you create in your home. With your behaviour you can create an aura of calm. Not a pretend calm or a side order of calm. You need to become so good at calm that it becomes the pervading mood in every interaction.

That calmness will in turn create a pattern of consistent, persistent parenting. But consistency takes a plan. A plan for the everyday and for the small shifts that will make a big impact. This is a plan that doesn't ask you to choose between strict discipline and having a great relationship with your child; between having a successful career and being a brilliant parent. And you don't have to spend any money to achieve it.

This consistency will reach its zenith in a positive, relational approach to parenting. It will give you the chance to be the parent you really want to be: caring and loving, while holding boundaries and successfully teaching behaviour. Through all the ups and downs, what is most important is your relationship with your child. Relational parenting respects that. It ensures that even in the trickiest moments, your relationship is never in question.

Calm parenting. Consistent parenting. Relational parenting. These principles form a concrete base for your parenting regardless of the age of the child. From these foundations, we will develop a completely new way for you to behave and for your child to behave.

We are going to look at why shouting is useless and why 'positive noticing' is a super-fuel for improving behaviour. We will look at how to teach new behaviours, structure routines and embed clear and simple rules. We will look at the small behaviours and work out how to deal with the bigger ones. I will show you how to plan for those tricky moments and how to celebrate the best ones.

We will look at scripts to use in response to poor behaviour and examine how best to respond to an angry child. There is advice on consequences and punishment, with an emphasis on protecting relationships. We'll cover restorative conversations to help you to repair things when trust is broken, and I will walk you through a plan for getting started on your own protégé today. And we are going to do all of that without blame on the parent or shame on the child.

All of these tools can be used by any parent of any stripe. When I talk about 'family' in this book, I don't mean anything exclusive. The focus is almost always one child working with one adult, be they mum, dad, foster carer, family member or friend. Whatever the family type – gay or straight or co-parented or single-parent or anything else – that basic building block remains the same: one adult, one child, how they communicate.

This approach is not just more inclusive. It is also more effective. Even if you have six children, it is always better to deal with their behaviour using the one adult, one child principle. Trying to manage children as a group – or too many adults dealing with a child's behaviour – complicates things unnecessarily.

I have also deliberately used a mixture of pronouns and ages throughout the book. The gender or age of your child does not affect the principles outlined here. The focus is on your behaviour, not the stage of development of your child. Change yourself to change your child, be they four or fourteen.

Along the way, there will be moments when you recognise yourself in some of the examples, and feel the cold shudder of 'That's me, I do that.' This is not intended to embarrass you – it is to show just how common some of the most common mistakes are. You aren't the first to make them. Although I would love you to be the last.

AN APOLOGY

And so it is that I find myself writing a parenting book. For which I must apologise. After all, this is not a situation with which I am entirely comfortable. I would ordinarily rail against being given parenting advice. I certainly haven't presumed to give any to my friends (I wouldn't dare).

This is not driven by my own ego or some obsessional desire to be invited to go on *Lorraine*.* I have learned from making all the mistakes, ignoring all the advice, and then finding the humility to listen and understand. I was not born with magic parenting skills. I learned from brilliant teachers, parents, social workers and mentors. I am as fallible as you and often more so. I am here to help.

While I'm at it, I would also like to apologise to my wife and children, who frankly don't need the grief of having a husband/dad who writes parenting books. Should this book take off, I am of course ready and willing to change their

* Although I would rock it, obviously.

names, fly them to Panama and put them in witness protection when the *Daily Mail* comes for me.

But first, there are changes that you need to make. There is much that will need adjusting in your home. All of it completely doable. Starting with the most important step of all: a pledge to stop shouting.

CHAPTER 1

THE LAST SHOUT

Emotionally regulated adults and how to become one

Let me give you the opportunity to have your last shout. One more for the Gipper.

It needs to be a good one. Don't hold back. Open the window and shout at the world/moon/irritating neighbour mowing their lawn at 7 am. Put your head under the water in the bath and scream. Pop into the car, turn up the radio and give it all you've got.

Good. Make that the last time you waste so much energy on something so utterly redundant.

Anger is not an effective way to relate to your children – or, for that matter, to yourself. Raised voices tempt confrontation and trigger angry responses. They erode the self-esteem of your child, cause anxiety, and even promote poor future behaviour. I would like them to be as socially unacceptable as pushing into the queue at the Post Office.

You need to be the person who is the calmest, the most rational, the most restrained. Even with teenagers who appear to be on the edge of your control. Even with young children who don't seem to understand reason. Even in your weakest moments.

Shouting is not part and parcel of being a parent. It is a decision. If you want to change your parental behaviour, the first step is to find a way to keep your emotions in check. It is learning how to be an emotionally regulated adult.

FALLING OFF THE WAGON

Most parents know all this already. They know that shouting doesn't help. They know that the dream is to be a Zen-like monk, nodding silently and sagely as chaos erupts all around.

Everyone with children has experienced this struggle. When my youngest was two, we drove from our home in London up to Oxford. It was not a particularly long journey, and one that in ordinary circumstances would be delightful. Alas, my youngest was going through a phase of crying and screaming for long periods. It was difficult to work out why. It is possible that he simply liked chaos.

That morning, he didn't want to be in the car or in his car seat. The moment we pulled out of the drive he turned into a wailing banshee. For an hour we did everything we could to calm him down – distraction/Pom Bears/offers of cold hard cash-money – but none of it had any positive effect. In fact, we probably made things worse.

I am usually reasonably good at ignoring such outbursts. But this time was different: the noise was incessant and loud and penetrating. In the end, we were only two streets away from our destination when I snapped. I pulled the car over on a side street, climbed out, and with as much drama as I could muster, shouted at full volume, 'I AM NOT GETTING IN A CAR WITH THAT CHILD EVER AGAIN!'

There was a pause. My partner gently pointed out that it was going to be difficult to accommodate that request if we ever wanted to travel anywhere as a family. Ever again. She suggested that we finish the journey, considering we were literally yards from our destination. I sheepishly got back in the car, muttering to myself, and drove on. The screaming continued.

None of us is perfect. I am a long way from being so. Yet lots of us have had the sensation of being unbelievably patient for long periods of time, then snapping and exploding inappropriately at the most unexpected moments (e.g. 50 metres from their destination). Every parent has had these experiences. Every parent has beaten themselves up about them. Every parent has tried to come up with a strategy for beating them. But most of these strategies don't work because we never get to the bottom of what is causing us to erupt in the first place. Trust me, I've been there.

BUTTON-SPOTTING

What is going on in these moments? Well, they have a lot to do with the part of your brain that regulates your emotional responses. Your amygdala is designed to keep you alive by reacting to perceived life-or-death threats. In modern life, it often causes a life-threatened overreaction to events that are not life-threatening at all.

The strategies your brain offers are not sophisticated. It forces you to decide between running away, standing up and fighting, staying motionless to avoid getting eaten, or simply submitting and giving up. When faced with an angry bear, you might want to take one of these options. When faced with a frustrated child, you probably need to upgrade your response.

The emotional mind plays havoc with your ability to be rational and consistent. But if you focus your energy on controlling your emotions, rather than trying to control the child, you will soon be taking steps forward.

That process starts with working out why your child is causing such a disproportionate response in you. Do you know which buttons they are pressing? Do you even know what those buttons are?

The way we raise our children is inextricably linked to our own worries, guilt and deficiencies – we project our anxieties back onto our children, and see ourselves in their behaviour, so much so that their behaviour can appear to be a direct reflection of our parenting. Sometimes it might feel as though your children don't love, like or value you as a parent, which can be a trigger for many. It means that your response to poor behaviour is loaded with the fear that you might be the worst parent in the world. You aren't. But you do need to work out what drives you nuts and why, so you can recognise it every time for what it is.

In some cases, this is a trauma response. Parents might have experienced their own physical or emotional trauma as children. They may be hyper-vigilant towards perceived threats. As a result, their amygdalan response can be off and running before rational thought has had a chance to put its trousers on.

If you are someone who had to rely on this response to keep safe as a child, it can be hard as an adult to react less instinctively.

More often, it is a fear reaction. Or rather a 'FEAR' reaction: False Expectations Appearing Real. We project our own absurd fears onto our children. So the child stealing an illicit hour of late-night gaming sparks a cascade of false expectations. The worry accelerates from 'They cannot be trusted' to 'What else have they been lying about?' to 'She'll end up in prison for fraud, I just know it.' Whether it's your three-year-old sneaking an extra biscuit or your fourteen-year-old slipping off to Notting Hill Carnival, before you've had a chance to do anything practical to find them your mind is filled with dread: are they overdosing on jerk chicken or being abducted by a knife-wielding axe murderer or joining a sound-system crew and escaping to Kingston, Jamaica.

These fears that your child will take the wrong path are strong, and rightly so. Parental worry begins as soon as your child is born and lasts a lifetime. But you can stop it affecting how you deal with their behaviour.

It will take a little time, but the better you know your buttons, the less proddable they will be. Very soon, there will be no attraction to your child in pushing them at all. They don't seem to work anymore.

THE HABITS OF EMOTIONALLY REGULATED ADULTS

You can work out what your buttons are through some focused self-reflection. A little research into your own behaviour. For five days, note down every time your response to your child is instinctively emotional. You will find that regardless of the context, there are certain behaviours that cause you to respond with an almost automatic harshness. Most are obvious, repetitive and predictable. You will probably end up with four or five main categories and a tally chart.

Make a note of when your emotional buttons get pushed. Are they more easily poked when you are tired, overworked or overwhelmed? Write down the time of day when you wobbled. Do it properly and by the time you get to day five you will be reacting differently anyway. The very act of self-reflection means that your conscience will kick in and start to remind you.

Once you've spotted these buttons, you can start to get rid of them. But that is not always straightforward. When your buttons are being prodded incessantly, the lure of a shout can feel irresistible. And yet you know that you are capable of stopping yourself exploding, because you often find yourself in places where emotional outbursts are not acceptable. You have the resolve to not scream 'You can shove your job up your . . .' at your boss when she's sending you micromanaging emails. You have the patience to not bellow in the face of the man who's very slowly scanning his vegetables at the supermarket self-service checkout.

You already have the ability to control your emotions. You just need to apply that ability when dealing with your child.

Your child, obviously, is not your fellow shopper – or even your boss (though it might sometimes feel like it). Everything about parenting is personal and has the potential to be an emotional minefield. 'If you keep doing that I am going to scream'; 'That tapping drives me nuts'; 'I can't handle you leaving the lights on, it makes me so angry.' Their every decision seems to expose your bad parenting, and what they do becomes tied to how you feel.

So more than at work – or the supermarket checkout – you need to give yourself time. Learn to pause. When you feel your emotions rising, allow yourself a moment. Try 7/11 breathing (breathe in through the nose for a count of 7 and out through the mouth for a count of 11) to bring your heart rate down. Try taking a second to completely relax your thumbs* (the focus on something else, even for a moment, helps you zoom out from the chaos). Waiting is not weakness.

Try it now, while you're calm. Breathe in and breathe out. Imagine stepping back from a situation and think through how it would feel. The strategic pause must become your default in moments of high drama. So default that soon, nobody will think anything of it.

REHEARSING FOR THE BIG NIGHT

Once you've developed your strategy, practise it. Unless you rehearse keeping cool, you won't be able to maintain it in the hardest moments.

Think of yourself as an actor preparing for their big break. You are learning your lines for the lead role: the emotionally regulated adult. Soon the audience (your child) will be

---

* I still can't do this one myself, admittedly.

throwing roses at your feet, while you take standing ovations from the neighbours. For now, rehearsal is everything.

In practice, that means running through the difficult moments in your head. Go back to your list of buttons and think about how you feel when each one is pressed. Approach the difficult moments with foresight. How will you respond?

With enough rehearsal, you can eliminate almost anything that might give away your emotional response. Watch yourself in the mirror and try to replicate your usual physical reaction. Strip it all out. The screwed-up face, the tut, the shrug, the kissing teeth. Remove every scintilla of aggression and frustration. Every hint of anger, every shard of irritation. Every frown, every pursed lip, every eye roll.

Then focus on your tone. Say the words out loud to yourself to see how they sound. Now, do it again, but take the harshness from them. See if you can make them more controlled, less confrontational and more kind. Imagine you are speaking to your child while their teacher is listening in. Choose a tone that you would be happy to use in public.

Now think about the words themselves. Rehearse what you *want* to say the next time you feel your emotions rising. The language you use needs to be non-combustible. Stick to the facts, avoid blame, shame and judgement. You can learn to be the most reasonable parent, even in the most unreasonable of circumstances. Eventually.

We'll cover all of these areas in more detail later. For now, just think about them for a second. You can learn to be unshockable and immovable in the face of poor behaviour. You can learn to park how you feel and show your child a rational response to their behaviour. Your emotion will only taint that pathway.

You are rehearsing the role of the perfect, emotionally regulated parent. Eventually, you will forget that it was ever a part you had to pretend to play.

Five ways to stay in control

- *Before you intervene, stop.* Take a moment to read the situation and think about how you can reach the outcome that is best for everyone.
- *Don't judge the situation immediately.* It is easy to judge first and ask questions later. But instant judgement encourages a defensive response from the child and gets in the way of the real lesson. You can't teach properly if you rush to conclusions.
- *Postpone decisions.* Particularly when it comes to consequences. Get used to saying, 'I need to think about what happens next' or 'Let's come back to this later' (more on this in Chapter 8).
- *See difficult moments for what they really are.* Nothing more than a test of your own behaviour, your own control and your own ability to regulate yourself.
- *Reward your successes.* Every time you successfully manage a situation that you would previously have laced with emotion, give yourself a pat on the back. There is a real sense of pleasure and accomplishment when you find that there is another way, and it is better for everyone.

PAVLOV'S DINNER BELL

You also need to think about which daily habits have an inadvertent shout-inducing effect, even if it's only incidental. In some families, emotions escalate through superfluous yelling. Yelling not for the sake of anger, but for the sake of convenience.

In these homes, shouting is a remote control. It means you don't have to move from the spot. You can bellow orders and assume they have been listened to, internalised and acted upon. You are absolved of responsibility and the child will be at fault if they haven't immediately done as they're told. Better, you've saved your legs from the journey up the stairs, into the TV room, along the corridor.

But there can be unforeseen consequences to this. The first shout might be casual enough. The second will be more urgent. The third time you shout, it is full-blooded and always tinged with irritation. This usually elicits the response 'What?' or 'Why are you shouting at me?!' or 'I WAS WEARING MY FUCKING HEADPHONES!!!' In seconds, everyone has lost their cool.

Shouting is a false economy. You save a few steps in the moment, but those savings have a poor payoff. So embrace the maxim, 'We don't shout'. Stop using the remote control. Get up, walk to where you need to be, and speak, not shout – even if it is simply to share the good news that dinner is ready. When you go and talk to the people you need to, you cut the raised voices in your house immediately. Requests will be calmer, followed with more grace and performed with less grunting. Everyone will get used to speaking face to face.

Of course, there are times when it is not possible to spend ten minutes patiently rounding everyone up. For those occasions you need a simple hand-bell, like the one you might have seen your primary school teachers using in the playground.

Now bear with me. A bell is loud, instantly recognisable, and doesn't rely on a digital interface or people deciding when they want to read a message. Start the association between the bell ringing and food being served as early as possible in your child's life. Ring it before every meal, even when the child is still in the highchair. Repeat the positive connection between bell and food and your children will come running every time they hear it. This takes the stress out of trying to finish cooking and calling people to the table.

It also means that you are deliberately conditioning your small human to the bell. This is going to be extremely useful if you need to speak to them about the state of their room/ why they haven't done their homework/why there is a soft toy hanging out of the window on a noose. Once the routine of the bell is embedded, it can be used to summon children for all sorts of reasons.

Don't overuse it, mind. If used sparingly for non-food-related reasons it will be accepted. Particularly if there is a spare biscuit at hand to reaffirm the bell/food trigger. Ring it constantly and the bell will lose its magic.

KNOW WHEN TO WALK AWAY, KNOW WHEN TO RUN

It might not always be possible to maintain a poker face. Your child reads you constantly and expertly. Even if you think you're controlling every physical cue that might reveal your frustration, if you are seething on the inside you will inevitably give yourself away.

Micro-expressions are hard to hide. These are the non-verbal cues that are signs of stress, frustration and anxiety. A furrowing of the brow, a twitch at the corner of the mouth, a biting of the tongue. In difficult conversations it is likely that your child will be hyper-vigilant. They may be searching for any clue that might leak out about how their behaviour has affected you.

If your micro-expressions reveal your true emotions, then the child will see that you are struggling to stay calm. They see you being controlled and yet uncontrolled.

So there will be times when you need to walk away from a conversation to protect everyone. But don't flounce out. Explain that you need some time to consider what to do next. Leave all your options open (so not 'Right, I am going to go and devise the most evil of punishments to serve upon you!'). Work out what helps you to pause, regroup and react with calm serenity. Practise regulating yourself, even in the middle of a crisis.

In this time, reframe the incident in your head before you try and tackle it. Zoom out a little. What is this really about, and why has it irritated you so much? Which boundary is the one that you need to underline? How can you deal with the behaviour without attacking your child's character? What is the outcome that would be best for everyone?

Rationalise what is in front of you. Resist the urge to allow your emotions to take over. This is just behaviour, just a moment. It signifies nothing and it is not a sign that you are a dreadful parent.

It might even be an opportunity. A chance to see if that bloke who wrote that book is right. First principle: when the parents change, everything changes.

TESTING

- Challenge yourself to go a week without shouting. Just a week. No 0–100 mph, no loudly issued rebukes, no disproportionate oral explosions. If you can do a week, you can do two. Maybe more.

WHAT TO WATCH OUT FOR

- Falling off the wagon. You might shout once or twice in the beginning. Don't let a bad day sour your resolve. Climb back on and walk yourself through how you might react differently next time.
- Linking not shouting with not intervening. You must still address poor behaviour, but in a different way. Don't step back from your usual standards. Just enforce them with no hint of annoyance, frustration or panic.
- Thinking that you have cracked your own emotional regulation in a few days. Like anything, it needs practice and a commitment to calm every day. Your emotions can unexpectedly hijack your rational approach at any time. Emotional regulation is a daily challenge.

NUGGETS

- Create a calm space where you can keep your emotions in check. For many that place is the bathroom, but I hope there are better options too. Use your calm place when behaviour is wobbly and emotions are high. Keep a note there of why you have chosen to take control of your emotional responses, and remind yourself each time you are on the edge.

- Try looking at yourself in a mirror after an emotionally intense moment. See if you can spot any physical cues that might give away your response. Then practise: adopt a poker face for correcting behaviour and check your body language.

- Sleep and emotional regulation are old friends. The more rested you are, the calmer you are. I realise that if you are currently co-sleeping with a three-year-old, an unwell ten-year-old and the dog, that you may not be able to solve the lack of sleep problem, and frankly having it pointed out to you over and over is not helping . . . ok, ok I'm backing away . . . but if you can get more sleep, grab it and increase your peace.

CHAPTER 2

THIS IS HOW WE DO IT HERE

Consistent parenting done properly

A lot of parenting is improvised. Responses to poor behaviour depend on the day, the mood, the amount of sleep you got last night, how empathetic you feel, how many times it has happened before, how many coffees you have or haven't had, and a million other variables.

This is a risky business. Making it up on the spot might feel like free-form jazz to you. To your child it feels unpredictable and inconsistent.

Unpredictable adults don't feel safe to children. They are difficult to trust and give irrational messages about behaviour standards. One day, military discipline is expected and new routines are introduced. The next, every poor behaviour is ignored. The next, there is a tsunami of emotion in response to the most innocuous comment. Children start walking on eggshells. In a desperate attempt not to provoke the adult, their behaviour changes. They become secretive, sneaky, focus their energy on not getting caught.

None of this is desirable. None of it teaches great behaviour.

Children need to feel emotionally safe in their own home. That means they should experience responses that are calm and predictable. Consistency is key. It is what builds a sense of nurture; one that doesn't stop when they go to school, or even when they hit the teenage years. A well-nurtured child – one who is used to having a place of safety – finds it easy to be resilient, explore the world, take measured risks.

Without a plan for consistency, angry and chaotic parenting can quickly become normalised, and children learn to cope with the unpredictability. They often find unorthodox ways of getting some control of their own – and when they battle for control while you are trying to do the same, conflict is inevitable.

If you want to transform the way your children behave, they need structure and boundaries and to feel safe and loved, consistently. This isn't a temporary fix: it needs to be a long-term plan that develops and grows as they do.

You need to define 'How we do it here'. It will identify the consistencies in your home and keep everyone on their game.

It isn't a list of punishments and rewards. It is much more useful than that.

HOW WE DO IT HERE

Imagine a sign hanging over the front door that says 'This is how we do it here'. The behaviours that work for you outside of these walls are not in your direct control. But when you walk through that door, everyone knows: 'This is how we do it here'.

Define it. Agree it. Stick it on the fridge if you want to.

When I say 'This is how we do it here', I'm not referring to a simple list of rules and routines. Nor a series of mantras and scripts for what to say, when and how. These can be useful, and we'll get onto them later. But for now, our focus is on something more basic: the culture in your home. That is what 'How we do it here' describes.

When behaviour wobbles, come back to this culture and use the mantra to refocus everyone. 'We don't do it like that here, remember?'; 'No, you can't take your food upstairs, that isn't how we do it here'; 'We don't say "Bollocks" to Granny here.'

Use 'This is how we do it here' to notice when your child is doing brilliantly, too. 'Thank you. That is how we do it here'; 'You did that without being asked. That is how we do it here'; 'Well done for carrying that safely. That is how we do it here.'

It is an endlessly flexible motto, adaptable to any situation. It requires no improvisation or freestyling skills.

With 'This is how we do it here', your child gets the same response on a Monday morning as on a Friday afternoon, regardless of your mood, your caffeine intake, or the phase of the moon. It is crucial that the responses are the same every time. All of the hard work spent establishing consistency in your home can be undone very quickly otherwise. It is too easy on a tired Sunday morning to permit behaviours that conflict with 'how we do it here'. In the moment, it might seem like the easy option. After all, everyone wants a quiet life, and it is Sunday, and last night was a little rough. Come Monday, we wonder why we are having to renegotiate long-established agreements, and why by Wednesday there is a full-scale mutiny.

'This is how we do it here' is also the perfect parry to the constant cry of 'My friend's parents let them eat on the sofa/vape in the house/inhale a packet of Percy Pig sweets before dinner/stay out until 5 am/drink Monster for breakfast/poke the dog with a spatula.' It means you are able to defend the standards in your own home without being pulled into impossible parallels with others. 'They may well do it like that at their house, but this is how we do it here.'*

'This is how we do it here' seems easy to establish. But like all consistencies, it needs to be ground out every day until it becomes just a normal part of daily life. The climb is hard, but the joy of reaching the plateau is worth the effort. You will know when it has landed properly as you will overhear your children telling their friends when they come over, 'Mummy's make-up in the blender? Not sure that is how we do it here.'

PARENTING CONSISTENCIES

It is easy to get 'This is how we do it here' wrong. A culture comes not from a detailed spreadsheet (don't do it) that maps out every behaviour and situation (seriously, no) – but from

---

* It is interesting that everyone else's parents always seem to be free-loving liberals with no boundaries, who sleep when they like, smoke reefer at dinner, and spend at least sixteen hours a day in front of a screen. Of course, they are better parents than we will ever be. Imaginary ones always are.

consistent behaviour from the adults. Changing the atmosphere in your house starts with you.

So it falls to you to work out what your own culture of consistency looks like. Start by thinking about how you plan to respond to common problems – children not following instructions, being rude, or not cleaning up after themselves. Instead of fighting specific fires, try and think a bit more strategically. Sketch out a plan. We will unpack these broader categories in later chapters in more detail, but for now just start thinking of a couple of answers to each question.

- How do the adults behave?
- What are the values that we live by?
- What are the key routines?
- How do we deal with conflict?
- How do you want the climate to feel?

Once you have some answers, stop and write them down. Get your expectations out of your head and onto paper. The goal is to make sure that your expectations are always clear. Your consistency depends on it. Rather than teaching your child what the right behaviour is by telling them when they slip up, give them the information up front. All of it. Make it look like you planned it, and like it didn't come from a quiz in a book.

This will require time. It takes persistence to grind out the consistency you need. If you are reading this as new parents, you have time to plan. Phew! If you are reading this because your behaviour strategy hasn't worked, then you need a plan and some steely determination to create consistency from the chaos. In this case, it will be small steps, but ones that you never need to backtrack on. You aren't going to turn things around in twenty-four hours; it is going to take weeks and months.

Planning might feel like something you would do at work, not at home. But it is vital. Without it, the outcomes for your child will be a crapshoot.

Five areas of consistency

- *Consistent expectations.* The standard of behaviour that you expect from your child should not be greater than the standard expected of the adults. Define your expectations. Make them simple, clear and easily translatable to any situation.
- *Emotional consistency.* Being emotionally available when everything is going well is easy. Sustaining that through the tricky moments is harder but something to work on. If you are frustrated, irritated or angry, then it is likely that you will find it hard to empathise or even read your child's emotions accurately.
- *Audible consistency.* What are the things you say to bring your child back to the rules (on which, more later)? Those same phrases need to be returned to again and again. When your child says to you, 'Alright, enough, I know the rules,' you know that this audible consistency is beginning to bear fruit.
- *Consistent routines.* Routines save time and discourage conflict. Once learned, the process is agreed upon and conduct is accepted. Behaviour becomes automated.

As we'll see later, there is work to be done to initiate a new routine – but as a result there is no longer lengthy negotiation or correction needed. They are simple, logical and make life predictable.

- *Consistently calm.* When behaviour is poor and people are feeling wobbly, it is important that a calm process is used to resolve things. When you have an agreed way to deal with conflict that includes calm steps that aim to restore and rebuild relationships, everyone knows what to expect. You will no longer be searching for the biggest punishment but the best conversation.

RUSHING TO JUDGEMENT

Hasty decision-making is the enemy of consistency. Sometimes, you need to take a second to step back and reflect on the basics of 'This is how we do it here'. If you respond impulsively to every situation you encounter, those basic consistencies are immediately trashed.

Every parent has experienced this. We have all had moments when a rush to judgement has left us with egg on our face, an upset child and an apology to make. The trouble is that our immediate perception of events lets us down, often at critical moments.

As a young teacher, this rush to judgement caught me out many times. I remember talking to a group of older students who I didn't know well and who viewed me with intense suspicion. As I walked away from them – after the familiar discussion about 'where they should be' and 'what lesson they have next' and 'can I smell smoke/vape/alcohol or just another Lynx deodorant flavour?' – I heard one of them tell me to 'fuck off'. Spinning around, I immediately identified the culprit, Ismail, and marched him off to the headteacher's office. We were followed by the rest of the group, all loudly protesting that I had the wrong man and on the verge of hastily recording a protest song and launching a petition.

Arriving in the headteacher's office, slightly flustered and out of breath, I explained that I had been the victim of 'abusive language' from this child. The headteacher, in full and unwavering support of his new colleague, decided to send Ismail home and began drafting a letter to his mum – although he did remark that this was surprising as Ismail had never received so much as a detention. I left the office and walked past the assembled agitators, confident that justice had been done.

At the end of the day, I was asked to pop back to the head's office. I assumed it was simply to ask after my welfare following a difficult day. It wasn't. It was to ask me again who had told me to fuck off, and how precisely it had happened. I felt a little put out that my judgement, which had initially been accepted, was now being questioned. I explained again, but realised that my back had been turned when I heard the comment. As I'd spun around, it was Ismail who was laughing and who caught my attention immediately. I had assumed it was him, and that the swearing was directed at me. I had assumed wrong. The other children had patiently explained to the head that the swearing wasn't from Ismail and that it wasn't about me at all.

I had managed to falsely accuse one of the nicest, most dedicated and humble of students. His friends were all of equal stature, and far from being the regular suspects hanging out in the corridors during lesson time they were in fact waiting for a member of staff who had asked them to volunteer for a special project.

A disaster. My rush to judgement had almost led to an incorrect exclusion from school and had certainly damaged my relationship, reputation and consistency in the eyes of these students. It took a long time for that damage to be repaired, and they always took great pleasure in reminding me of my 'youthful enthusiasm for punishment'.

Being quick to judge has no benefits. Once again, the solution is to stop. Pause. Allowing time to think and not forcing yourself to make urgent decisions means better and more consistent outcomes. It also means that you don't make promises you can't keep or threats you won't follow through on. Your consistency depends on rational decision-making, not heat-of-the-moment responses that you spend the rest of your day / week / life apologising for.

BUYING TIME

So get used to using some stock phrases to slow your natural rush to judgement. Each one carves out a little time for you, without you appearing indecisive or weak. If you deliberately use 'I' and 'we' rather than 'you', it removes any chance of your child feeling you have already made up your mind.

'I need to think about what has been said' is better than 'I need to think about what you just said.'

You need this time to reflect on what has happened. A little perspective is very useful, particularly when things are getting heated.

Very quickly your child will get used to both the mantras and the pause. They will see it as a footballer sees VAR. It is a space to allow you time to see things from every angle before you look to solve the problem.

These phrases allow you to remain consistent, even when you don't have a clue what to do. They give you the chance to think, 'Right, this isn't going well, what am I going to say to turn it around?'

You will make fewer mistakes. You will find yourself apologising less, and not having to repair damage so often.

CO-PARENTING CONSISTENCIES

I once worked with a huge sixth-form college that had a very specific difficulty: students wouldn't stop sitting and eating their lunch in the corridors. It was a problem. There was food all over the place, legs in the way when people needed to pass, and constant confrontations between staff and students.

We agreed a consistent, almost scripted approach for all staff, and that nobody would just walk by any corridor-munching miscreants, ever. The teachers were to stop, politely challenge the students, and invite them to take their pot noo-dles/weird Japanese snacks/prawn cocktail crisp sandwiches and move outside. Within a week, things had improved dramatically. Staff reported fewer students eating inside, less litter, and freedom of movement returning to the corridors. By the end of the second week it felt like they had cracked it.

But it was a false dawn. A member of the senior leadership team was spotted walking past a large group of students sitting in the corridor eating their lunch. The news spread like wildfire. As colleagues heard the story, a significant number also gave up their consistent approach and started walking past. They reasoned that if the leadership were not going to intervene every time, they felt no need to. By the end of week three we were back to square one, the corridors cluttered with students, plastic food and inconveniently placed legs.

This isn't a million miles from the dynamic between some co-parents. Consistency means holding the line, whether you are in a college of 2,000 students or in a home of two. Co-parenting is a team sport.

Gaps in your consistency are easily exploited by children. There is space created for mischief. Disagreement can be used to gain an advantage, from playing one off against the other ('But he said I could'), to preparing pathways to divide the two of you ('Did you ever stay over at a friend's house when their parents were away? Because my dad says he did').

If you want to provide a consistent climate in your home, there needs to be a plan in place. Your shared understanding of 'How we do it here' is essential. Get all your ducks in a row first, before attempting to draw boundaries for your child.

The same applies for separated parents, even if things are acrimonious. Adults who are incapable of communicating create chasms between them, allowing the child an unhealthy amount of space in which to play unregulated. Guilt might mean that children are showered with gifts and cash, while the level of upset in both parties renders them useless as emotional role models. Some children grow up very quickly in the gaps between their parents. This, coupled with the standard separation–attachment trauma, is enough to ruin any consistency that was established previously. The child is left to make a lot of it up by themselves – often to grow up by themselves – while parents use them as collateral in their endless pursuit of one-upmanship.

But that doesn't mean parents who are together are off the hook. Here too, friction between the adults can complicate things. Consistency should never depend on how the grown-ups feel towards each other day to day. Being annoyed with your partner is an occupational hazard in any relationship. But you can't allow it to affect the way you deal with your child.

Your child needs a consistency that rises above the ups and downs of the dynamic between the adults. Just because you are seething that your partner has loaded the dishwasher like a chimpanzee, your child doesn't deserve your emotional backwash.

PICKING UP YOUR OWN TAB

The most important principle for co-parenting consistency is that each parent deals with the behaviour in front of them without deferring to the other.

As a young teacher, I was always amazed that children who were removed from my room had to answer to a higher authority, and never to me. I recall working in a notoriously tricky school where behaviour could easily get out of hand. One day, a gentle request for David to remove his coat escalated rapidly. After schooling me at full volume as to why he wasn't going to 'Take his fucking coat off for anyone', he ran across the tops of the desks like a ninja warrior, kicked a hole in the store cupboard door and jumped out of the window (fortunately, we were on the ground floor). He proceeded to sit on top of the headteacher's car until the head looked out of his window and promptly suspended him from school.

Watching this drama unfold, I knew that his punishment would be delivered in a meeting just opposite my classroom. So I decided to go along. After all, it was me who was going to have to teach him again – and it was me who would again have to ask him to take his coat off tomorrow morning.

I knocked on the door just as the meeting was getting started, and it was opened, just a fraction, by the headteacher. 'What do you want, Mr Dix? We are about to start an important meeting.'

'I wondered if I could come in. You see, it started in my lesson and I want to make sure—'

'No, Mr Dix,' he said. 'This has gone way beyond you.' And he shut the door very slowly in my face.

It had taken me a long time to establish my authority with David. I didn't need someone else to deal with his behaviour. Their hierarchy wasn't helping me to establish true consistency with my pupils; it was undermining me.

Parents create these hierarchies too. When you pass responsibility for dealing with your child's behaviour to your partner, you are undermining yourself. 'Wait until your mum / dad gets home' is buck-passing. It means someone else is higher in the hierarchy.

That isn't as great for you as it sounds. Forcing one parent to be bad cop doesn't mean that the good cop gets away scot-free. Don't be surprised when your child starts responding quicker to them than to you. They might even look over your shoulder to see when the person who is really in charge is coming. You don't want that.

It is a lot of work to constantly pick up your own tab. Particularly if you have been used to someone else doing it. But it is never wasted effort. It is an investment in the child that always pays back. If you constantly delegate the difficult bit to someone else, your relationship with the child will never develop. Your parenting depends on it.

CO-PARENTING NIRVANA

Picking up your own tab raises questions. You and your co-parent are not the same person. How do you maintain consistency? Tolerance for poor behaviour can never be perfectly consistent between two people. It is easy to tie yourself in knots trying to remember what consequence is supposed to follow each misdemeanour.

So scrap the long lists of Response 31.6.2 to Behaviour 408c, and instead focus on the consistency of your emotional response. Calm, measured and rational. Every time. If your response is consistent when your tolerances waiver, nobody gets hurt.

Soon, your child will realise that the rules are always enforced by both adults individually. And when children realise that they are always going to be answerable for their behaviour, their behaviour changes. They stop running from one parent to the other or trying to avoid consequences. They stop being rude to you or thinking your instructions don't matter. When you pick up your own tab there is no need to seek a 'higher authority' or to suggest to the child that one even exists. Hang a sign around your neck, buy the t-shirt, or preferably get the full chest tattoo: 'The buck stops here'.

8/10

At this stage you might begin to reflect on your own inconsistencies and simultaneously give me the side eye. To expect every parent to be completely consistent 24/7 is not realistic.

You are right. We all have our moments. I have more than my share. The good news is that you don't need to be a 10/10. An 8/10 is good enough. Get it right 8/10 times and you will appear to be consistent, reliable and, perhaps most importantly, predictable.

If you can be calm, consistent, slow to judge, on plan and on point 8/10 times, your child will forgive you for the two occasions when you respond with frustration or behave slightly irrationally.

So when you do fall off the wagon (and you will), don't use it as an excuse to binge-shout every irritation you have been holding back, list all of your child's faults or issue three-dozen cruel and unusual punishments. Just dust yourself off and get back on the horse. Recognise your slip-up, apologise if you need to, and return to your plan. Your default settings are what matter. 8/10 is consistent parenting done properly.

TESTING

- Start with dinner. Does everyone know 'How we do it here'? Notice the key areas – when we can start, how we pass dishes, how we show we have finished, what we do if we don't like something, when we can leave the table, and which topics are not good for discussion while people are eating. Better, when a guest comes for dinner, ask your child to explain to them how we do it here. Does everyone understand the culture you're trying to create?

WHAT TO WATCH OUT FOR

- Overcomplicating things by making a huge list of expectations that nobody can even remember let alone follow. The confusion will fuel inconsistency.
- Overemphasising parts of the agreement that are not yet being followed perfectly. Build confidence in your agreed consistencies by highlighting the successes in the first instance. Don't let poor behaviour fog your view of the good stuff.
- Taking your eye off the ball by thinking that 'How we do it here' has become embedded. It takes time, particularly if it's a fairly new framework.

NUGGETS

- Write down your shortlist of 'How we do it here'. Agreements that are not written down are just wishes. Do it with your child alongside you if you like, but don't allow your standards to be diluted; it is, after all, your house.
- Establishing and embedding consistency means grinding it out every day. You can't afford to let the bindweed of old ways to start growing and taking over. Clear your personal bindweed every day. Don't allow yourself to get pushed off the path.

CHAPTER 3

POSITIVE, RELATIONAL PARENTING

You get more of the behaviour you notice most

The ultimate solution to your child's behaviour lies in your relationship with them.

The idea of consciously building a relationship with your child might seem odd. Many assume that the relationship with their child is automatic. That the genetic connection is enough, or that all that nappy-changing, feeding and being weed on gives you the right to a relational nirvana.

It is easy to imagine that your child will forgive you for anything. They won't. If your behaviour plan is built on the idea that your relationship is unbreakable, then it has bad foundations.

To make your relationship with your child as strong as it can be needs your constant, careful attention. Just like every other relationship that you have. Strong relationships are not accidental or circumstantial. They change and often fail when you stop working on them.

With your own child, that work rests on everyday habits. It isn't in grand gestures ('I know I haven't spoken to you for months but we are going to DISNEYLAND tomorrow!') or big talks ('You may only be six, but we need to talk about your life choices: have you considered chartered accountancy?'). Relationships are built on small, daily actions.

Above all, they are built on the elements of your child's behaviour that you choose to notice. You can focus on rules and boundaries as much as you like – but it is what you comment on that most affects a child's internal monologue. How you talk to your child matters. What you notice about their behaviour matters most of all.

POSITIVE NOTICING

If your parenting antennae are always scanning for examples of mistakes, mess and poor behaviour, then you will find it. Constantly. If they are set to notice your child behaving well, correcting their own mistakes and clearing away mess, you will find that constantly, too.

This isn't a magic trick or a positive-thinking self-delusion. When you notice the good stuff and tell people about it, you change your child's thinking. Catching your child doing the right thing is so much more impactful than catching them doing the wrong thing.

Tell a child they are naughty, bad, chaotic, aggressive, difficult or trouble often enough and they won't just believe it, they will filter every single thought through it. Drip, drip, drip.

Tell your child they are determined, diligent, resourceful, creative and kind and they will start to reflect it. Drip, drip, drip.

The goal is consistent, daily noticing. You get more of the behaviour that you notice the most. Labels stick. Labels applied by parents stick harder.

In time, what you notice gets picked up by siblings, other family members and even random strangers ('Ooh, she is naughty, isn't she?'; 'They are terrible at that age'; 'Those are the eyes of an axe murderer', etc.). Soon enough, everyone surrounding the child is filtering their opinions through what you pick up on. A bad label will affect every relationship they have, however casually it was created.

You need to make sure that every label that lands on your child is a positive one. You need to make sure that everyone sees your child through a positive lens.

Positive noticing does not just matter during childhood. Its effects can last for years, even decades. Bad labels are judgements made in a moment and perpetuated, sometimes, for a lifetime.

A friend recalls her 89-year-old nan, who felt she had failed in her life. She would constantly refer back to comments on her school reports that she 'could do better'. It left her with a lifelong impression that she hadn't ever done anything well. The truth, of course, was that she had achieved a great deal – this was obvious to everyone who knew her. She just could never see it for herself.

What you say to your child really matters. Because the way you talk to them is how they will talk to themselves. Repeatedly pointing out their faults does not bestow an internal monologue that anyone would want their child to possess. The stories you tell your children about themselves shape their self-image, and their future.

NOTICING THE SMALL STUFF

Positive noticing means picking up on the small stuff.

A few years ago, I went to a petrol station and paid as usual. I wasn't really concentrating when I gave my card to the cashier (this was before touch payments) and was busily scanning the confectionery section for a jumbo Double Decker. As he returned my card, he said very casually, 'Thanks very much, Mr Dix.' I was a bit taken aback. I wondered if he might be an ex-student. 'How do you know my name?' I asked. Of course, he had just read it off the card. I must have handed my card to thousands of people, but he was the first to pay attention and use my name.

He made me feel important. Just for a moment. I guess he must do it to everyone, but it hasn't happened to me anywhere else since. I tell everyone about that small kindness. A small, seemingly inconsequential thing, yet one that had an impact way beyond that moment.

That is what positive noticing is all about. It doesn't need to be theatrical. There is no need to roll out the pantomime dame, 'Ooooooh, didn't he do well?' Or to fill your home with never-ending cries of 'GOOD JOB!', 'NICE WORK!' or even (dreadfully) 'WAY TO GO!' This isn't a time for cheese, it is a time for sincere, honest observations. Make it low key. Simple noticing often starts with the simple things: 'I like the way you . . .'; 'You are really good at . . .'; 'I love that you . . .'

If you are like most parents, you can probably recall many moments when you have praised your children. But how regularly do you notice the small stuff? It is minuscule, almost inconsequential noticing that builds the positive self-image that we all want our children to have. Notice, let it land, and then move on. It mustn't feel awkward or sound forced. Casual, almost throwaway, is best.

'That is lovely.'

'I noticed how much effort you put in.'

'Thanks for being so kind.'

'Just love the way you do that.'

'You always do that so well.'

Positive noticing needs to be regular. If it helps, aim for ten positive acknowledgements a day. Get some in early, before breakfast; a few after school; a couple before bed.

Do it for just a day and notice the reaction. I don't think you will want to stop. It is lovely to live in an atmosphere of positive noticing. Small things, regularly noticed, are the tiny bricks that build your child's confidence.

STICKY PRAISE

Positive noticing doesn't take the place of other praise; it adds to it. Sometimes, you will want to go further. But if you are going to make the effort to praise more and criticise less, then it is worth considering how to get the most out of it.

The goal is what I call 'sticky praise'. It is sincere, specific and directed. It takes a little longer than simple noticing. Sticky praise doesn't just notice the behaviour; it explains why you are noticing the behaviour and relates it to the agreements you have made about 'How we do it here'.

'I noticed that you did your homework already. Thank you. It really helps when you take control of things yourself. I love that you are respecting our agreement. That has made me smile.'

It is worth lingering a little in this way two or three times a day. You are simultaneously reinforcing good behaviour and 'How we do it here'. You are teaching behaviour through the good moments when your child is keen to listen to you.

'Hey buddy, great job!' isn't sticky, it's just annoying. 'Wow! Here's a reward point for you!' is patronising to anyone above the age of five (more on this in a minute). 'You are amazing, a child genius, a modern-day miracle' might be a little over-egged.

Instead, try: 'Thanks for clearing up after your baby sister. It was a real mess. I appreciate it. You are really good at looking after her. I am proud of you. That is how we do it here.' It is sticky in the best possible way: recognising the effort that has gone in, offering a positive label, relating it back to the expectations in the house.

Tell your child why you are praising them. Out loud and up front. Don't let the positive thoughts remain unspoken. Tell your child what the praise is for and how it reflects well on them.

Sticky praise builds relationships, while also building a good self-image and clear boundaries. Being on the receiving end of it is a better feeling than money can buy. When it is delivered by the people whose opinion matters most, it is life-changing.

Four positive moments to start today

- *Notice when the child makes an effort that is over and above.* This is behaviour that is beyond minimum standards. It covers brilliant things that your child does without being asked.
- *A positive minute before they leave for school.* Just a little pause before you set off. Take a moment to notice the good stuff and to frame the day for and with your child. 'Thank you for being ready on time, it really helped that you packed your bag last night. I feel like you are going to have a great day, you have already given me a positive start.'
- *Reflect on the good stuff when you sit down and eat.* Get in some early positive noticing to set the climate immediately: 'Thank you for coming to the table on time / I noticed you gave up your seat, love that / I saw that you waited until everyone had their food before starting, perfect.'
- *Notice the day's positive behaviours at bedtime.* Bedtime is a great opportunity to reflect on positive behaviour. Don't be tempted to lace it with the negative moments. Just let them lie. Let your child go to sleep knowing that they are valued, appreciated and loved.

PRIDE PATCHES

The pictures of children that most often make it onto the wall at home are the super-smart school photos, the staged shots, the most memorable moments from many years ago. They are the photos that evoke the most powerful emotion: pride.

Pride is a remarkable motivator, the stickiest emotion of all. Along with positive noticing and sticky praise, you can evoke it with your actions.

If you want to give your child evidence of their ability, values or effort, take some pictures of them in their most naturally positive moments: studying hard; standing proudly in their newly tidied room; being gentle, kind and respectful. Show them their best side every day.

Let them face their confident, generous, humble selves as they walk to the bathroom. Show their kind, diligent and courageous sides in the hallway so that everyone notices. When they doubt themselves or have a bout of imposter syndrome, these photos will remind them how capable they really are. Simply by hanging in the background, they offer a way to reframe problems and act as a constant positive reflection.

You don't need to redecorate. Just a few well-chosen images in the right places can work wonders. Make your home a gallery of proud moments and surround your child with the best versions of themselves.

There are other ways to build pride into the fabric of your home. Recognising when their conduct is 'over and above' is what your fridge door was made for. Clear off all the coupons and terrible drawings so that you have a place for instant recognition.

A simple piece of paper is enough. It doesn't need to be elaborate. Each time you notice your child going over and above, just write their name on the paper, or a smiley face, or a rainbow. Set a target and when your child meets it, celebrate it.

A recognition fridge is particularly useful when you are establishing new routines or trying to convince your child that they are able to behave well. The visual reminder is powerful and every aunt, uncle, friend or grandparent who visits the house also gets to reinforce the positive.

Your fridge should be a constant reminder to everyone that your child's default behaviour is fabulous. That is a great foundation to build on.

YOUR OLD HABITS

If you are someone who does notice your children's good conduct but never voices it (or puts it on the fridge), the changes described in this chapter might feel odd. Speaking your positive thoughts isn't always easy, at first anyway. You will need to find a way that fits your style.

Many of us are hindered by our own past. Some adults can count the number of times their parents told them they were proud of them on their thumb(s). Restraining your natural urge to praise your child is part of a strange theory that they will appreciate it more when you eventually do so. It has given some people permission to acknowledge their child's good conduct once a year/once in a blue moon/just the once, on their deathbed.

The opposite of this approach is often to explode into a tempest of emotions when things go badly. You see this in bad sports coaching, where the response to defeat is anger and criticism, sometimes public. It is ugly to watch. I have coached sports teams where the opposition coach seemed intent on crushing the spirits of his under-eight team: a tirade of negatives delivered at the end of the game left everyone reeling (children, parents, even players on the other team). The monologue picked fault in every player, including you, yes you, what do you think you were doing out there, your defensive line was appalling. Fault correction becomes char-acter assassination.

If that is your routine, it is time for a change. We are taught to let sleeping dogs lie: not to interrupt when children are behaving in the right way, and to intervene only when trouble is brewing. But children are not dogs (not even sleeping ones). They respond not to passivity, but to positivity.

THEIR OLD HABITS

Your children might also struggle with your new world of positive noticing – at first, anyway. Remember, not everyone finds it easy to accept praise, particularly if it is too public, too frequent and too gushing. A child might need easing into this new style.

This is what I learned from Nelson. At thirteen years old, Nelson was not easy to have in class. When he arrived, chaos arrived soon after. He would storm in late, refuse to follow any instructions, smash a few things up and then run out of the room. I was a new teacher in a very tricky school but even I knew this wasn't right. I went to other teachers to ask for help and they instantly adopted a 1,000-yard stare. 'Ah yes, Nelson,' they told me. 'Nobody knows what to do about Nelson.'

I tried my best to notice the positive with Nelson but it wasn't easy. The rare moments that he did behave well were almost accidental. I remember giving him a couple of positive Post-it notes that I thought would make him feel better about himself. He just screwed them up in my face. My behaviour was making no difference at all, I thought.

One day, after a particularly difficult lesson in which Nelson had destroyed his own work, other people's work and my sanity, I resolved to 'sort him out'; an odd expression, but the one that was running around my head. I was cross. Everyone seemed to have given up on speaking to Nelson's mum – 'She never answers the phone, doesn't respond to messages, nobody knows what is going on' – which irked me. How hard could it be? I decided I was going to go and see Nelson's mum.

As I marched down the school drive with my new motto, 'I'm going to sort him out', echoing around my head, I had a crime sheet of all of Nelson's misdemeanours to relay to his mum. As I reached the end of the school drive, a colleague I got on well with joined me. 'I am coming with you, Paul,' she said.

'I don't need you to.'

'Yes you do,' she replied.

As we approached Nelson's house, I ran through the speech I was going to give. But as soon as his mum answered the door, my preconceptions were fatally floored. I had somehow imagined that Nelson's house was the same as my house, that Nelson's mum was the same as my mum. Instead, I entered a house without furniture. Everything had been sold or taken. There was just a two-seater sofa piled with clothes and random toys, and a two-bar electric heater blaring out heat on a hot day. Nelson's mum made me a cup of tea, but you wouldn't drink it.

Undeterred, I perched on the end of the sofa and was about to deliver my speech. That was when I noticed that Nelson's mum was drunk. Pie-eyed drunk. Her eyes were rolling. It was 11 am.

I froze. I was a young teacher and didn't have enough life experience. I just didn't know what to say. My colleague, Sue, a famously excellent head of year, took over. She knew Nelson's mum of old and expertly diverted the conversation to remove any awkwardness. 'Did I see you at the Bingo on Friday? It's not been a great week for Nelson . . .' And they were off.

As they were talking, Nelson approached me and said he wanted me to see his room. As we trudged up the stairs, I found myself wondering why he wanted to show me. He had never shown much interest in my opinion in class. When we got upstairs, I remained perplexed. There was no furniture in Nelson's room either. Just a mattress on the floor, and piles of clothes. And then I noticed them. Just above the mattress there were two pieces of paper blue-tacked to the wall. Two pieces of paper that had been scrunched up and unfurled. They were the two positive notes that I had written for him.

As we walked out of the house, I found myself apologising. 'I'm sorry, Sue, I didn't realise. Have I made things worse?'

'No,' she said. 'But don't expect instant miracles.'

The next day, Nelson came into class and stayed there. We never mentioned the home visit or his mum. But our relationship had taken a different turn. Mine was the only class he stayed in.

The positive notes were important to Nelson. He had wanted me to see them in his room, had wanted to show me that they mattered to him. He still wasn't able to accept praise easily, or public praise at all. But this was one step along the road. Perhaps the first step in him understanding that praise and appreciation were safe and encouraging and sincere.

Those notes were the beginning of me learning how to teach Nelson properly. But I learned something else, too. That positive noticing might be working even when it appears not to be.

RELATIONAL CURRENCY

With time, these small acts of positive noticing ripple out across whole relationships. They are the small acts of kindness that define how you relate to a child.

Think of these moments as creating relational currency. Build your currency reserves every day by appreciating your child's efforts. That means turning up at school to share the important occasions. Turning up at sports events, especially if they are losing. Turning up not only in the good moments, but also when things are going badly and they need a hug of reassurance. Put as much currency into the relational bank as you can.

When things go wrong, when your child struggles to regulate, when you would normally issue a punishment, it is the relational currency that you can turn to. The stronger your relationship, the easier it is to correct behaviour without threatening consequences or raising your voice. When everything is going wrong, it is what can come to the rescue.

Take Altaf. Some children lose their temper. Some seem to almost lose themselves. When Altaf lost it, nobody could bring him around. It was exhausting to watch, and people who got in the way were likely to end up hurt, physically or emotionally.

Altaf fought a lot. I am not sure that he really enjoyed fighting, but he was good at it, and it was an effective way to keep the other children wary of him. He had built a reputation as a hard man and wasn't about to give it up in a hurry. Not because he was a skilled fighter or a particularly strong one, but because he was utterly relentless. Other children were frightened of him because he never gave in and wouldn't stop. Ever. If they messed with him, it wasn't going to be over quickly – and it wouldn't end well.

So it was that I found myself in the middle of an altercation between Altaf and the 'top boy' from the neighbouring school. I had seen the crowds gathering and looked around for other members of staff. They were nowhere to be seen. It was a tense situation and, if it went the wrong way, people would get hurt, me included. A fact that was obvious to the other staff, who were now watching the whole thing unfold on a CCTV camera monitor in an office with a cup of tea and a custard cream.

I didn't enter the situation lightly, but Altaf and I had known each other a long time and had had many ups and downs. He had confided in me about his heroin addiction, which was serious and advanced. Once, I stupidly left him in my car for five minutes on his own – whereupon he stole my car stereo, ran into town and sold it for a hit.

So I decided I owed it to Altaf – and to our relationship – to stand between the two and try to stop the fight – putting myself directly in the line of fire. By this point, Altaf and his counterpart were squaring up to each other, with me in the middle.

And so I played the only card I had left. I looked at my shoes and said, very calmly and quietly: 'It's not happening here. Not now, not with me in the middle of it.'

And then, after a pause, 'Nice shoes.'

There was a moment of silence. Then Altaf said, with a smile, 'Stop it.' And then he walked away.

I was cashing in my relational currency because it was all that I had. It broke the tension well enough. I knew I couldn't use it again for a while: what had been spent needed to be replaced. But without it, things could have gone quickly downhill. And with it – and to the bewilderment of my colleagues, who had gleefully imagined having to scrape me off the playground in the aftermath of teenage violence – I emerged in one piece. I never did thank them for their unstinting support.

You cannot lean on relationships like this too often, of course. The default must be to try and bank relational currency, not spend it daily. Otherwise you will soon find yourself bankrupt. Save it for a rainy day and it will have immediate impact and be transformative. Lean on your relationship to try and correct every behaviour and it won't work

But used right, it can be transformative. Even if you have reached the depths of poor behaviour and verbal abuse, start finding the good stuff. It might take some time to build up a healthy account balance for those in the most difficult situations. But it is always worth starting to save. If you have enough relational currency in the bank, you can get through anything.

Seven ways to build relational currency

- *Offering help.* Where you previously would have offered threats of punishment.
- *Turning up.* To support their interests, even when you have important things to do.
- *Sitting with them through homework.* Rather than just insisting it is done.
- *Breakfast in bed.* When it hasn't been asked for and wasn't expected.
- *Secret snack in the school bag.* With a positive message alongside.
- *A jar filled with bits of paper.* Each one with something you have positively noticed this week.
- *Helping to tidy their room.* Instead of just nagging them to do it. And having a lovely positive conversation while you do so.

CARROT-DANGLING

When I talk about positive noticing, many parents think I mean offering rewards: 'If you do X, there's a dangling carrot/pack of Tangfastics/PlayStation 5 waiting for you.'

In fact, this is the opposite of building relational currency. Your goal is to nurture your child, not pay them off. Rewards very quickly become bribes. It is a short hop from 'Here is a treat because you were brilliant' to 'If you are brilliant I will give you a treat' to 'Ok, three treats for each piece of clothing you pick up' and then to '£100 cash for every A grade.'

One of my friends has a drawer of wrapped presents that she uses to bribe her five-year-old. Getting into bed, there's a present for that; tidying up clothes, there's a present for that; screaming for a present, oh yes, there is a present for that. The drawer now empties far faster than it used to, and the presents are constantly upgraded. But the five-year-old has not learned anything other than how to get better presents faster and with less effort.

A drawer full of presents is expensive. More importantly, it doesn't work. Once you have embarked on this road, behaviour becomes transactional: good behaviour in exchange for a material reward, rather than as an end in itself. Worse, it starts to affect the child's expectations of life. If every good behaviour resulted in material reward, then nurses would be driving home in gold cars wearing Prada shoes. Life isn't like that, unfortunately. When the rewards have disappeared, what is motivating them to behave well as adults?

If you want to prepare your child so they behave brilliantly when you are not present, then teach them to feel good about their behaviour. You need to encourage your child to have pride in doing a good job, being polite and treating other people well.

It is not the extrinsic rewards that drive great behaviour but the intrinsic ones. They need to behave well because it is right, not because there is a wrapped present behind your back or a crisp tenner in your palm. Avoid the temptation to reinforce every moment of positive noticing with a custard doughnut/novelty-flavour Oreo/nomination for a knighthood. Your child doesn't need it, and it will just complicate a situation where simplicity is required.

What works better than bribery, money and prizes (and is considerably cheaper) is acknowledgement, recognition and pride. This is why positive noticing beats all the bribes that you can invent.

TESTING

- Notice something small tomorrow. Don't treat it as hugely important, just notice it gently and calmly. Then notice the same thing the day after, and every day for the next week. Watch the change, watch the questioning, watch the confidence growing.

WHAT TO WATCH OUT FOR

- Too much too soon. Relational parenting is drip-fed every day, not achieved in one 'bonding' trip to B&Q.

Start making changes slowly, and make sure they are sustainable. Don't try and do it all in a week and imagine you can then stand back and just watch your child behave perfectly.

- Overwhelming your child with lots of gushing praise in public. They won't know how to deal with it and may not be able to accept it gracefully. You don't want a positive shift in your behaviour to embarrass your child (although it is, I know, entirely possible to embarrass your teenage children simply by being present / within 100 yards / alive).

- Turning the taps on too quickly. If you are someone who finds it difficult to praise naturally and suddenly become the World's Number 1 Positive Noticer, you will doubtless appear to have undergone an overnight personality transplant. 'Have you been reading that behaviour book again?'

NUGGETS

- Imagine your child leaving home on their way to school with a big brown Paddington Bear-style label tied to them that flaps in the wind. What would you want it to say? Make these your last words to your child before they walk out of the front door.

- Repairing a relationship can take longer than you expect. It may not happen just because you suddenly do something kind and generous. Relationships are not immediately transactional; don't expect a positive response just because you are making an effort.

- Small kindnesses are great distractions. Just bringing your child a drink before sitting down to talk can break the tension. A gentle reassuring hug, even when a conversation might be tricky, can make all the difference.

CHAPTER 4

THE COUNTER-INTUITIVE PARENT

Why crush behaviours with punishment when you can grow new ones with love?

Teaching a child how to behave is counter-intuitive. What feels like the right response in the moment is often driven by emotion. And in managing poor behaviour, emotion is not your friend.

The pull to respond to your child's behaviour with frustration or anger is natural. You barely need to think about it. Child stays out late, you stay up late to read them the riot act. Child refuses to follow instructions, you snap back at them. Child throws a cup, you tell them why someone will inevitably die from their cup-throwing violence.

These instincts are the enemies of good parenting. Don't let your impulses drive your behaviour. There is simple logic waiting just behind them, ready to bail you out.

This relentless return to reason offers a better way to teach behaviour; one I call counter-intuitive parenting. It is how you turn the ideal of emotional regulation that we explored in Chapter 1 into a set of hard tools that can actively teach new behaviour. When you feel the tug of your emotional response, you can learn to recognise it for what it is and reach for the rational alternative. At first it's counter-intuitive. You soon wonder why you expended so much emotional energy simply teaching your child how to behave.

Resisting these intuition traps is simple but transformative. Once you stop responding to poor behaviour with emotion, you become fairer, more predictable. You deftly skip around the emotional bear traps that end up making things worse, and life calms down significantly. The result is a different way of getting the behaviour you want; one focused not on crushing or bribing away the bad behaviour, but on actively teaching the good.

Don't worry if you realise some way through this chapter that you may have been down a few wrong paths. Relationships will heal and repair. You can be successful from wherever you start. Even if you have taken a few wrong turns, there is always another way.

TURNING OFF YOUR FACTORY SETTINGS

Intuitive parenting is at its most powerful when we are pushed for time, frustrated or irritated. In these moments it is easy to say things that you don't mean, and with the wrong emphasis. Your linguistic defaults kick in, and suddenly you find yourself posing ridiculous questions that you were asked as a child: 'Who do you think you are?' or 'How many times have I told you?' or the endless 'Why don't you listen?'

We all have our own factory settings. They have been planted through endless repetition, often by our parents, sometimes by our teachers. They leap out of our mouths when we stop thinking about our words and mean we end up dealing with present difficulties using clichés from the past. A conversation about behaviour is not the moment to launch into deep philosophical questions about existence and identity ('Who do you think you are?'). It is time for a plan.

Allowing the voices of your own parents to come through – in the form of your defaults – means that you are not in control of what you are saying. You will find yourself in conversational cul de sacs that are entirely of your own making.

When used thoughtlessly, our factory settings will teach children that their behaviour and character are one and the same. That their behaviour is an unchangeable characteristic rather than a temporary blip. The same phrases and behaviours come up again and again – all intuitively likely to teach better behaviour, all vanishingly unlikely to do so.

INTUITION TRAP 1: 'YOU SHOULD KNOW HOW TO BEHAVE'

What is striking is how many of us fall, slapstick, into the same old intuition traps. Consider a classic: 'you should know how to behave'. This line seems to be hard-wired into every parent. After all, you taught your child how to behave at least once, perhaps in some detail (and yes, the PowerPoint with transcription was overkill). So now 'they should know how to behave'. Shouldn't they?

Unfortunately – and don't blame the messenger – teaching behaviour is not a one-off gig; even if that gig was your very best performance with accompanying visual aids and dry-ice effects. Teaching behaviour is more like one of those gigs that you have to perform seven days a week, including matinees and late nights. Teaching a child to 'know how to behave' is a deliberate act that takes months, even years. So each time the thought 'you should know how to behave' flashes across your mind, suppress it. It's an emotional, intuitive response. The rational response is 'I need to reteach them how to behave'.

This is something I learned in the classroom. As every teacher will tell you, just because you have taught it does not mean they have learned it. You need to teach and then reteach every day until the behaviour becomes the default. That might sound like a lot of effort. It is. It is also unavoidable. If you want to teach your child how to behave, you need to put the work in.

When your child doesn't know 'how to behave', that means you haven't taught them well enough. This should be an internal frustration, not one reflected back at your child. Don't blame yourself, just work out a better way to teach it, so they actually learn it.

When teaching new behaviours, the first step is to apply the principle we encountered in Chapter 1: eliminate the emotion. Counter-intuitively, less emotion has more impact on poor behaviour. As soon as you allow emotion into the driving seat, the exchange becomes about your behaviour as much as your child's. The less emotional you are in tricky situations, the more impact you will have and the better parent and behaviour teacher you will become.

INTUITION TRAP 2: CRIME SHEETS

In the wobbliest moments another impulse is to reach for the crime sheet almost immediately. 'This is the fifth time this week that you have . . . '; 'You are always . . . '; even 'This pie chart represents the number of times you have told me I am a boomer in the last 24 hours.' Behaviour seems to be cumulative and recorded fastidiously.

Often the crime sheet is used to justify the severity of response or to ramp up the shaming: 'I spoke to you about screen time yesterday, on the 24th, and twice on the 17th: at 0737 *and* 0738. It is therefore time to stamp on the iPad'. 'We've been so nice to you recently: most notably yesterday, on the 26th and, in addition, on the 12th. And all you do in response is this.'

But past evidence doesn't help improve today's behaviour. Keeping a list of your child's worst moments is not healthy, even if it is only in your head. This too is emotional, not rational, behaviour. None of it is helping. It is just an oversharing of your sense of helplessness and frustration.

The crime sheet is particularly ineffective when you are correcting behaviour that is happening right now. It says to the child, 'I have already judged this situation, found other instances of the same and therefore you are to blame' – before any conversation has taken place. There is no justice in such an approach and your fairness will become the most contentious point; suddenly, you're not talking about the behaviour itself, you're talking about the bias of your response.

Here, too, intuitive parenting is your enemy. Impulsively, yes, it makes sense to list examples of the same thing happening before: this is the case for the prosecution. But is a child really going to learn how to do something because of the weight of the evidence against them? 'Yes, Dad, I have listened to you present the case against me and agree that I am guilty on all counts. I intend to immediately cease being rude, donate my pocket money to the swear box and go to my room to give myself a good talking to. Oh, and I would like another twenty-three swears to be taken into account.' This is not how real people think.

If you are keeping a crime sheet for your child, you need to dial down your impulses. Stop, think, and compare and contrast with the adult world. Who keeps check on your behaviour? Who adds to your list of misdemeanours every day? In the adult world, behavioural mistakes don't accumulate. There is no one with a clipboard keeping score; if there was, you would either call the police or ask your old PE teacher why they are still following you.

Nobody ever decided to behave better because someone kept a list of their slip-ups. Crime sheets simply taint the conversation and confuse the lessons you are trying to teach.

INTUITION TRAP 3: TOKEN ECONOMIES

For many, the desperate search for a solution to issues with their child's behaviour has led them to a simple idea: token economies. Giving children stickers or points that build up to large rewards should work. It feels intuitive. We all like a reward, and getting children to earn things sounds like a valuable life lesson.

In fact, token economies unravel very quickly. These systems are corrupt by design.

If a sticker-and-reward system works in the first few days it is because the adults are looking for the positive behaviour and are giving lots of positive attention: it's the positive noticing that's having the effect. Adults then delude themselves that it's the shiny toy at the end of the process that is causing the change in behaviour.

In the short term, this may even be true: the excitement of reward can, for a bit, provide powerful motivation. But their enthusiasm doesn't last for long. The motivation is extrinsic, not intrinsic. The result is a rapidly escalating inflationary crisis. The tokens lose their value. 'Oh no, Mum, this week I need two chocolate bars, a trip to the cinema and a weekend in Naples with pizza included.' By week four, the rewards have no effect whatsoever: 'I don't want a bloody ice pop, wash the dishes yourself.'

There's a more practical issue with token economies. Running an accumulator for rewards takes a lot of effort. First, you need to work out what behaviour equals one token. Next, you need to work out how it scales. 'Ok, so washing the car is five tokens, being nice to your brother one token, and not telling your granny about the thing we agreed is thirty-seven tokens.' And that means consistency goes out the window. Soon, the chart is not being updated with any consistency, if at all. Worse, if there are two people operating the system, consistency becomes an impossible dream.

So the result of token economies is not better behaviour. It is behaviour games. Children don't think about how perfectly they can behave to earn rewards. Instead, they immediately try to work out how to play the game and win. What is the easiest way to get a reward? Which token-master is more biddable? Who can be tricked into giving multiple tokens for the least effort?

Sound familiar? It's because the strategy is wrong. Don't blame the players, blame the game.

You know rationally (if not intuitively) that adults aren't motivated by reward schemes for long either. That is why your wallet is full of random points cards that you stopped collecting after the first purchase. It is why people leave toxic jobs, even if the sales bonuses are astronomical. Getting more stuff doesn't change behaviour for the better, much less teach it.

So tear down the reward-scheme pyramids. Clear out the wrapped presents that were dangled as bribes. Change your approach to rewarding your child. Motivation is counter-intuitive, too. Life isn't a constant exchange of rewards for good behaviour, so you need to send your child out into the world without a reward dependency. When their intrinsic motivation drives their behaviour, then the behaviour becomes the reward in itself. Your child feels good about themselves without the need for constant external validation.

Sticker charts are not the path to enlightenment. They are buying today's good behaviour but investing nothing in future behaviour.

Four more common intuition traps (and what to say instead)

- *'Stop that!'* Sharp interruptions are sometimes necessary for safety reasons. If your child is about to climb out of the window, you will want to get their attention as quickly as possible. In reality, though, using someone's name is the fastest way to get their attention. And most sharp commands are not the result of a child attempting to master flight from a first-floor window; they are (surprise!) your emotional brain firing off again. Instead, try: *'Remember our rule about . . . ?'*

- *'If you do that again . . .'* Trying to show someone they have made a mistake by daring them to do it a second time rarely ends well. At the end of the phrase 'If you do that again . . .' is always the threat of a disproportionate punishment (on which, more later). And when the threat doesn't work, there is little road left. Having invoked your most fearsome punishment, you will be forced to enact it – and then what happens if your child *does* do it again? Instead, try: *'Next time, let's . . .'*

- *'I give up!'* Proclaiming that you 'give up' is not a good message to send to your child. Of course, the statement is just an indication of your emotional exasperation. I am sure most parents aren't actively planning a life as a childless hermit as a solution to their parenting woes. To an adult, 'I give up' is just a figure of speech. To a child, though, it can be interpreted very differently.

It means that the boundaries are not being enforced anymore: another opportunity for the child to gain a little more control. If you wonder why the power balance in your relationship is shifting, it might well be because you are voicing your helplessness. Instead, try: *'Let's go back to our agreement . . .'*

- *'Look what you made me do!'* The transference of blame from the adult to the child is a truly awful parenting strategy. Often through no fault of the child, they are asked to feel shame for things that were never in their control. 'Look, you have made me ruin the dinner/kick the dog/miscalculate my tax return/spend next month's rent on Foxy Bingo'. ('But I'm only three!') No child has ever learned anything from this phrase other than that their parent is irrational. Instead, try: *'There are consequences to your actions . . .'**

GROWING NEW BEHAVIOURS WITH LOVE

All these intuition traps have something in common. They are trying to teach new behaviours. But they are doing so in a muddled, ambiguous way. The desired behaviour is never made explicit; it is hinted at obliquely via punitive sanctions/sprawling crime sheets/corrupt token economies.

There is another way. One that doesn't involve crushing the old behaviour with sanctions and gifts, but growing the new one with love. And it involves all the niftiest tools we've

* Proportionate ones, mind. See Chapter 8.

learned so far: emotional regulation, planned consistency, positive noticing.

First, be explicit about what you are looking for. Don't tell your child that they already know, or that they'll get twelve choc ices if they guess successfully. Just explain, clearly, the desired behaviour. Be specific. Focus on one single positive behaviour that you want to nurture and encourage. If you want to grow new behaviours, then aim for small, manageable changes.

It is best if this is an observable behaviour, rather than just 'change your attitude'. And one behaviour at a time is plenty. The positive behaviour might be 'Eating with your mouth closed'; 'Speaking to me politely'; 'Being gentle with the cat.' (rather than the negative: 'Argh that's disgusting'; 'Don't tell me to piss off'; 'No cats in the fridge'). Explain how behaving in this way helps you. Give examples of where and when it is important.

Ambiguity is your enemy. Asking your child to 'behave' is too broad to be useful or understood. Yet it is not unusual for parents to demand of their child to 'stop being naughty' or 'behave yourself' or even 'be good'. In these circumstances the child may not know exactly what that entails. So they use your emotional response as the barometer rather than addressing their own behaviour: 'If Mum isn't shouting I must be doing the right thing.'

Next, connect the positive behaviour that you are asking for with the values in your home, and with 'How we do it here'. And start noticing it, immediately. Look out for it. Comment on it when you see it, even (perhaps especially) if it is shown immediately. Let your child know how important adopting the right behaviour is. Thank them for making the effort.

Get every adult in the child's life to join in with your new bout of positive noticing. Ask friends/family/babysitters who interact with your child to look out for that behaviour. Make a fuss when it starts to be done automatically and without thinking. And don't start focusing on a new behaviour until the change is embedded, whether that takes seven days or thirty. You are nurturing the behaviour, with kindness and with love. It needs constant and gentle encouragement until the change is permanent.

BEHAVIOUR GAMES

Soon you will become the world's most dedicated amateur horticulturalist, growing new behaviours with love, care, nitrate fertiliser. But paradoxically, the very act of growing new behaviours with love throws up new intuition traps. These are the undesirable offshoots of your new approach. You need to do some pruning.

Chief among these offshoots are behaviour games. Such games start out with the best of intentions. There is a positive emphasis on noticing the good stuff, but it is easy to end up offsetting every 'good' behaviour against every 'bad' one. Resulting in a zero-sum game.

Take Chelsea. Her parents – good friends of mine – couldn't explain why, but by the age of seven everything with Chelsea felt like an effort. She needed to be reminded of the simplest things multiple times, every time.

At first, they did everything right. They began to spot the good behaviour and positively notice it. But it was slow progress. And there was still the question of what to do with the behaviour they didn't like. After consulting the world's most contradictory parenting guide, the internet, they alighted on a solution: a 'Special Behaviour Chart'. It was clearly a popular product, and the reviews were glowing. Forty quid seemed entirely reasonable if this was going to sort Chelsea out. They paid their money and awaited enlightenment.

On reflection it seems a little grandiose to call it a chart. It was a laminated piece of A3 card. It had two columns: one was labelled with a '+' to record good behaviour, and the other with a '−' to tally poor behaviour. There was even a pen so that ticks and crosses could be placed in each column. This, they thought, was positive noticing in action: you don't get much more noticed than a big green tick whenever you do something right.

Then, every bedtime, came the count. If there were more ticks than crosses, then Chelsea would get a reward. If there were more crosses than ticks, she would receive a punishment.

On the surface, all of this seemed entirely reasonable. It would be good for Chelsea to be accountable for her behaviour and take responsibility for her actions. The trouble was, the chart had no weighting for different behaviours. A tick was a tick no matter how impressive the positive behaviour; a cross was a cross no matter how dreadful the bad was. Slowly but surely, Chelsea learned that any good behaviour cancelled out any bad behaviour. This corrupted her behaviour and her response to it. It taught her how to play the behaviour game rather than reflect on her own conduct.

Things eventually came to a head when Chelsea was eleven. She had stayed out late with one of her friends. She was more than two hours late coming home – no phone call, no text. Both parents were hovering over the number for the emergency services when she walked nonchalantly through the front door. They both had the urge to have it out with her there and then, but resolved to ask her to go to bed and told her they would have a chat about this in the morning.

The next morning Chelsea was up early. They could hear her scrabbling around in the kitchen. As they looked into the room, Chelsea was chaotically wiping down the surfaces and trying to clean up. When she saw them at the door, she said, 'There! Look!'

'What?' her Dad replied.

'You can't get me about last night – look what I have done already!'

Four years of behaviour charts had left their mark. Chelsea's moral compass was so distorted that she truly believed that any good action would cancel out a bad one. It was, after all, what she had been taught for years via laminated sheets of perpetual accountability.

TEACHING BEHAVIOUR

You don't teach values through behaviour charts, even positive ones. If you create a ladder on which the child moves up a rung for 'being good' (hurray!) and down for 'being bad' (uh oh), with a prize or punishment at the end of the day, you haven't got a behaviour strategy, you have a game. The child will quickly learn how to play it really well. You will, of course, lose.

It also implies that all behaviour can be quantified, marked up on a scale of 'great' to 'ok' to 'bad'. In fact, some poor behaviour is off the scale appalling and can't simply be covered by washing the dishes or going to bed straight away when asked. Equally, some good behaviour is just brilliant and shouldn't be undermined by playing it off against the fact your child forgot to clear their cups from the bedroom.

Above all, this gamification has very little bearing on the real world. Imagine having to account for your own behaviour at the end of every day. There would be ugly scenes. This approach doesn't set a child up to succeed in adulthood, because adult life does not accord to its rules.

So (counter-intuitively) keep the good behaviour and the bad behaviour separate. The poor behaviour that the child is currently showing does not impact on the fabulous behaviour five minutes ago, and vice versa. The positives and the negatives must be distinct and unrelated.

That gives you the opportunity to talk and reflect on them without one being tainted by the other. It means you are really teaching behaviour: slowly, properly, rationally. Every time your child has a bad day, start looking for the positive moments and build on them. Soon the green shoots of positive behaviour will be poking out. Without a negative tally in sight.

TESTING

- The next time your child is behaving badly, pick out an example of them behaving well and start the conversation with that. You are not ignoring the immediate behaviour – you may need to come back to that – but for now you are simply noticing, positively, a more distant one.

WHAT TO WATCH OUT FOR

- Immediately picking up on the negative behaviour that is being offered to you. You get to decide when to deal with it. You don't have to react straight away. Sometimes silence is the best response.
- Getting caught up in the emotion. Particularly at first. There will be times when you will feel the pull of your intuitive responses overriding your rational, logical responses. These are moments to pause, leave the room, go for a walk.
- Passing the buck (even to me). You don't need to tell them that suddenly everything is going to change, or that renowned behaviour expert/lucky chancer/dangerous maniac Paul Dix says . . . Just change things slowly, incrementally. Without fanfare or credit to anyone else. These are your changes to own.

NUGGETS

- Thank your child before they have even taken action. 'Thank you for picking that up' works well: it assumes good conduct. 'Thanks for closing that door' is a gentler way to correct behaviour, even when they are old enough to know what you are doing. To increase the odds of your child saying yes, assume they are going to follow instructions and phrase your request accordingly. 'Thank you for taking your shoes off'; 'Thank you for sitting patiently'; 'Thank you for putting that dirty t-shirt in the wash.' It is a quick win that works surprisingly well.

- Children see, children do. Your model is more important than you imagine. Make sure that your own behaviours are always ones that you would want your child to copy.

CHAPTER 5

RULES REBOOT

You can be strict while being kind

I am sure that you firmly believe that there are rules in your house. But if you haven't defined them repeatedly, taught them incessantly and used them to frame behaviour daily, then it is unlikely that they are understood by anyone but you.

This is important. Boundaries must be understood by everyone before they can be properly respected. Waiting until your child steps over the boundary before teaching them of its existence is a common approach. The child never internalises the boundaries, nor understands why they are there in the first place. They just become used to being constantly corrected.

You don't just need rules. You need rules that live and breathe in your relationship every day. Rules and routines that are simple, clear and relentlessly taught.

Start with something simple. Ask your child if they know what the rules are. It might seem like an odd question, but you will be surprised at their answer. It will probably elicit bemusement ('The what?') or vagueries ('Well, you don't like it when I . . .' or 'You did shout at me when I . . . '). Your children are unlikely to know what your actual rules are because they have just picked them up implicitly. They might only exist in specific contexts, or never have been explicitly communicated.

Your challenge is to teach the rules until your children know them off pat, and think about them before they act. That means rules that are reiterated in every conversation about conduct, for a while at least. It means that every time you reinforce good behaviour or correct poor behaviour there is a context to your comments. You are not making up rules on the hoof or expecting your child to learn them on the fly.

Your rules won't just exist in one context; they will apply everywhere. You will save time, effort and energy. You will no longer have to justify why scotch eggs aren't allowed under the duvet every single time.

SIMPLE RULES, COMMUNICATED SIMPLY

If you are thinking of sitting down with your child and entering a radically democratic process of rule-making, let me save you some time. Just decide on the rules yourself. You are the adult; you get to set the boundaries.

When your child has learned the rules, they can certainly suggest changes. And you can politely decline. The rules are the rules. If you start flexing them because your child doesn't fancy them, there is trouble around the corner. When your child understands the rules, they have a secure and firm base on which to build better behaviour. Rules make children feel safe, even if they frequently challenge them.

If you want to sit down with your child and talk about rules, you can talk about what they mean in different situations. But you are not negotiating what they might be. Talk to your child about how the rules will help them to get things right, and what might constitute going 'over and above' in each case. Instead of inviting your child to create their own boundaries, help them learn how to stay within yours.

Counter-intuitively, it is not by creating the rules that your child will own them. It is by being taught them every day.

The trick is to keep the rules as simple as possible. Families often come up with convoluted documents outlining the rules in overwhelming detail and explaining how to apply them to every eventuality. The outcome is duly displayed on a poster in the kitchen, painstakingly coloured and replete with groovy acronym: 'BEHAVE – Be lovely, Eat properly, Have fun, Act cool, er, Very . . . something'. It is instantly forgotten, obviously. Soon, it is just another piece of artwork on the fridge, covered by takeaway menus and 'Granny is staying this weekend, defrost the lasagne, disinfect the dog' notes.

Even if it is stapled to the chocolate milk, it is not a poster that is going to do the work for you. It is your resolve to refer to the rules every single time. It is your behaviour that creates consistency for your child, ensuring that they know exactly where the boundaries lie.

GOLDEN RULES

Given the task of creating a set of rules, many families go for five. It seems like a nice round number, and surely five rules are perfectly manageable. In fact, even five is too many.

A headteacher once proudly told me that she had reduced her school's list of twenty rules down to just five Golden Rules. She had done two assemblies to each year group about the five Golden Rules in the last two weeks and was convinced that she had cracked it. 'We can do something else today, Paul,' she told me. 'We won't need to look at the rules at all.'

'Yes, perhaps,' I said. 'But I wonder if we could go and ask the children if they know what the rules are?' Reluctantly, she agreed – all the while insisting that everybody knew them – and we embarked on a hunt for a pupil. We soon came across a small boy lugging a tiny key attached to a huge wooden block towards the toilet. He was only six and was dragging the block down the corridor like a ball and chain.

'Look, I am an odd man and this is a strange question,' I said. 'But do you know the rules of the school?'

He looked confused and thoughtful at the same time, paused a moment, and then with real confidence exclaimed, 'Hats! It's hats, isn't it? No hats is one of the rules!'

'Margaret,' I asked. 'Is "no hats" one of the five Golden Rules?'

'No,' she said, somewhat deflated.

So we set off again, walking across the school and into a busy classroom of eleven-year-olds preparing for exams. I grabbed a quick moment with one of the girls. 'I am an odd man and this is a strange question,' I said, 'but do you know what the rules of the school are?'

She looked as quizzical as the six-year-old, thought hard, and then announced 'Hoods! The rule is no hoods.' The headteacher started walking away with suspicious briskness. 'Is it hoods?' I shouted after her. 'Is "no hoods" one of the Golden Rules?'

'No, of course it isn't hoods,' she said curtly.

'That is strange,' I said. 'Because the first child said hats and the second said hoods. So clearly you're getting some kind of message through to them.'

The reason, I gradually realised, was the weather. Northern English weather. This was Oldham. Even in summer it got chilly, and the children all came into school with their hats on and hoods pulled over their faces. And every morning, a group of staff members would greet the children by barking 'Hats and hoods' at them. They were the first words that the children heard every morning.

My headteacher had discovered the first rule of rule-making. The rules that matter are not the ones presented with a big fanfare. They are the ones that come most frequently from the mouths of the adults. That means it's hard to embed one rule, let alone five.

THE MAGIC NUMBER

The number of rules you are looking for is three. Threes are easy to remember, easy to connect with and easy to understand. As De La Soul once taught us, three is the magic number.

And your three rules need to be shorter than you think. You need to be able to fit them easily into the flow of conversation. Some rules are laudable but just too clunky. Try fitting 'Love thy neighbour' into a debate about homework: 'Look, I've told you before, love thy neighbour means doing questions four, five and six properly!' It doesn't work. If your rules are lengthy and too wordy, they won't be easily used in conversations about behaviour, and will soon be forgotten.

So your three rules should be represented by just three words. 'Kind, cooperative, calm' works well; I am yet to find a behaviour that doesn't fall within their scope, and they fit easily into conversations. You can go for different options, provided they are still broad enough to cover every eventuality and flexible enough to be mentioned every time. 'Caring, polite, gentle'; 'helpful, humble, honest'; 'dignity, humility, courage'. The three words you actually choose matter less than the frequency of use and your commitment to them.

Your goal is to weave these rules into everyday conversations as a matter of course. You don't need them emblazoned on posters all over the home. Instead, talk about the rules. At first, they will be prominent and emphasised. It might even feel a bit false and a real change of direction in how you talk about expectations. Quickly, they will just become accepted, understood and used to frame all of the talk around behaviour.

HOW RULES STRUCTURE LIFE

The rules should be everywhere. They should be present in the house and outside it. In restaurants, supermarkets and on the bus. They are not a temporary fix for a period of poor conduct. They are your forever strategy, easily portable and suitable for every environment.

The three rules offer structure to your everyday life. They give you three pegs to hang all behaviour on. Their role will become self-evident. Strangers may mutter in mild awe as they overhear you teaching, not just correcting or praising, your child. You may not want to be an actual teacher, but you are always teaching behaviour at home. Get used to referring to the rules constantly.

'When we go and see Violet we need to remember that she can't hear when we talk over each other. Our calm rule will be important.'

'As we are walking along the train platform we need to be considerate. What do we need to remember about that rule?'

'It's now 7.30 and we need to be ready to leave the house in twenty minutes. What needs to happen now so we can all follow the ready rule?'

The rules should be omnipresent, not only when you speak to your children, but when you talk about them to others. In your conversations with grandparents, aunts, uncles, cousins and friends about your child's behaviour, always frame it within the three rules. 'Amir is so *considerate*. When we went to the theatre there was an old soldier who just wanted to chat to him, and Amir's questions were so measured and respectful.'

This is a subtle but powerful method: it means that everyone around your child, consciously or unconsciously, is seeing their behaviour through the lens of your rules. Everyone leaves the encounter with Amir being 'considerate' fresh in their minds.

When your child gets this same message from multiple angles it doesn't take long before they believe it is part of their character. Drip, drip, drip.

ROUTINES THAT WORK

The rules are endlessly adaptable, but they are broad strokes. You need to work out what the rules look like when they collide with the realities of day-to-day life. This is where routines come in handy.

It is your routines that break down the rules for different situations. It is in your routines that the detail on how to behave lies. Getting your child to remember the rules is easy when there are only three. Getting them to remember how to act to satisfy those rules is more of a challenge. Routines give that structure.

My sister Sue is an accomplished dog trainer. She answers almost every question about dog behaviour with the same response. 'Barking too much?' Training. 'Not coming when called?' Training. 'Badly behaved around other dogs?' Training. The answer is training, every time.

Change training for 'routine' (and dogs for children) and it works just as well for parenting. I am not suggesting that you train your child like a dog.* But the answer to your problems is the same. Routines are training patterns for children.

That doesn't mean having a routine for everything. Routine overload is no fun. You need routines for the most frequent behaviour sequences, not for each and every occasion. Having 'the bus routine' and 'the walking on the pavement routine' and the 'going to Grandma's routine' quickly becomes overwhelming for everyone. They are impossible to remember, and the result is no routine at all. 'Remember the going to grandma's routine? No, neither do I. Look, just be nice, alright?'

The trick is to apply your three rules to the everyday routines that make up daily life. If your rule is 'Cooperative', this will mean specific behaviours when preparing for bed. Map them out for and with your child. You might decide that, in practice, 'Cooperative' means not trying to negotiate a different bedtime. You can then build this language into the context-specific routine.

These routines are your rules broken down into practical steps and/or behaviours. Take the following examples. Each routine is very simple; each is applicable on at least a daily basis; each of them is worth a week of your full attention to teach and reinforce properly. Each one is 'This is how we do it here' in action.

---

* Although I do wish I could housetrain my youngest to stop pissing on the toilet seat.

Five routines that deliver

- *Calm morning routine*
  - Out of bed promptly
  - Teeth and toast on your own
  - Dressed and packed by 8.10
- *Safe crossing the road routine*
  - Phone away
  - Headphones off
  - Heads up, eyes on the road
- *Practical home from school routine*
  - Put bag, shoes and coat away
  - Snack
  - 30-minute chill
- *Cooperative dinner routine*
  - Start when everyone is ready
  - Mouth closed when eating
  - Ask to leave the table
- *Calm bedtime routine*
  - Phone outside the bedroom
  - Clothes out (for the morning)
  - Lights off by 9 o'clock

WALL OF DEATH

Taught well, routines lead to behaviour that is pretty much automated. Children don't think about it. They just do it.

Before I became a teacher I spent a year as a teaching assistant, falling in love with the job. Endlessly earnest, I had more confidence than skill, and would gladly accept tasks that were way above my ability: offering to cover classes, coach the swimming team, lead outward bound expeditions, and so on.

In this phase of my career, it was not unusual for me to be asked to look after a class for a few minutes, or even to start a lesson before the regular teacher arrived. Usually, this was with the older children who were drilled to within an inch of their lives. However, on a day of high staff absence I had been asked to start a PE lesson with the youngest children. I remember thinking that five-year-olds would be much easier than the angsty adolescents I'd grown used to. I was wrong.

I arrived at the hall to see the children had already lined up and were waiting at the door. They were itching to get going, and I admired their keenness. I opened the door to let them in, just as I usually did for the older children, while simultaneously asking them to sit in a circle in the middle of the floor.

Except nobody heard that instruction. It was lost in the cacophonous excitement of the children entering a huge space. The class, set free in the hall, seemed like prisoners released after a month of solitary confinement. They zoomed around with their arms out, some skipping, some sprinting, some being aeroplanes, some flying dinosaurs. It was a tornado of five-year-olds with me in the middle.

As I bravely attempted to regain control, or even just the attention, of the group, I found myself encircled by a screaming and screeching wall of death. I used my loudest and most serious voice but it just seemed to act as encouragement. The more I shouted, the louder the children seemed. I blew my whistle, but it only elicited a communal whoop and accelerated zooming. Just as I was wondering how I would ever stop them, I sensed some people watching me. I turned around to see five faces squeezed into the small rectangular glass panel of the door. They were my colleagues, laughing hysterically, and they had been there long enough to see the whole drama unfold.

Taking pity on me, the head of PE strode into the hall, shouted 'Freeze!', and the thirty children screeched to an instant standstill. It was incredible and impressive and humiliating all at once.

Their routine was to wait for this cue. It had been deeply engrained in them and they had practised it every lesson. I didn't have the code, didn't know the routine, and so didn't have a chance.

TRAINING, TRAINING, TRAINING

This screaming five-year-old ordeal demonstrated that it isn't enough to simply introduce the routines. You need to teach them, relentlessly. Remember the dogs. Training, training, training.

This is not always easy. The most important thing is to set realistic standards. The children cannot be held to a higher standard of behaviour than the adults. If you are dragging yourself out of the house in your pyjamas while stuffing the remnants of last night's kebab in your mouth at 8.07 am (I'm not judging you, just saying . . .), then the example you set is invalidated. Children copy adults. Even the older ones who try really hard not to.

So take the time to identify what the routines are and what standards you will both stick to. Do this slowly and explicitly. When you want to change an existing routine, it can be helpful to map this out with them. Start with a few bits of paper and write down each step they are currently taking. Display them in front of you as you chat. 'When I ask you to do your homework, this is what happens . . .'

- Step 1: You tell me that you don't have any
- Step 2: You disappear for a while
- Step 3: You start doing some very involved task that is nothing to do with homework
- Step 4: We have an argument
- Step 5: After much upset and slamming doors, you go and do your homework
- Step 6: Teachers are not happy about the quality of the work and say it has been rushed

Now map out what will happen next time. Agree it, and write each step on a piece of paper so that it mirrors the last time. Put them side by side.

- Step 1: We check the homework situation together
- Step 2: You stay at the table and I will organise snacks
- Step 3: 20 minutes of silent work; set a timer
- Step 4: Quick check-in with me to see if you need help
- Step 5: 20 minutes of silent work; set a timer

- Step 6: We check through it together to make sure it is the standard your teachers expect

Finally, distil the new routine into three memorable steps, linked back to your rule: *Collaborative homework routine*

- Calm check-in
- Snacks and timer
- Silent work with support

When you first introduce a routine, take a moment with your child to run through any ambiguities. Ask some questions so that you can be sure they understand what is expected of them. 'Phone outside the bedroom' when going to bed seems clear enough, for instance. But where is the phone to be left and at what stage of the 'going to bed' routine? Ask the question and get clarification.

Now you are into training mode. Explain that you will remind them of the agreed routine if they need it, and will make sure they don't slip back into the old one. You can refer to the routine easily now: 'James, do you remember the new step 3?'; 'Chloe, brilliant, that is step 2, thank you.'

CONSTANT REMINDERS

Don't assume that because you have taught a routine once, that it is enough. Remember our Oldham headteacher: 'Just because you've taught it, doesn't mean they've learned it.' Teaching routines takes persistence.

So you need your own routine for reminding your child of their routine. A meta-routine, of sorts. And this routine needs to be a routine feature of your life. On this routine I can be a little more prescriptive:

- Pause
- Run through the steps of the routine
- Question for understanding

These reminders are a small investment of your time, every time. They help the child to recall and manage the transition. Again, ask them questions: 'We are going to need to cross this busy road in a moment. Do you remember what our "Safe crossing the road" routine is? What else do we need to remember when we are crossing the road? How will we stay safe? What is the first thing we need to do?'

In this moment, other distractions are put side. The routine frames what comes next and allows the child the chance to behave brilliantly. They know exactly what is expected of them. (The alternative – trying to intervene half-way across the road – is not going to go well. It will be tense and urgent and emotional.)

As the routine begins, notice and reinforce behaviours that have changed to meet it. Again, choose words and phrases that echo the routine.

'Oscar, thank you – that is exactly what we agreed for *step one.*'

'Lana, brilliant, you are already *moving towards bed.*'

'Lovely, Pranav, your *ready routine* is perfect.'

MORE TRAINING, TRAINING, TRAINING

The more you drill the routine, the quicker your children will welcome it, learn it and expect it. But it is important that you are not satisfied with a routine that is 'good enough'. Don't stop teaching it until you have it exactly as you want it. Make it seamless. Get the details right. Five minutes doesn't mean seven; asking to leave the table isn't just for the weekends, it is every time.

We are not looking for military-style drilling, but there is nothing wrong with being a bit picky. There is a reason those soldiers have such shiny boots.

With this in mind, it's imperative that the first routine you introduce is the most exacting of all. Whether you perfect it will determine the quality of every subsequent routine. If you start with a routine that is 'ok', it will quickly become 'meh', and then it is a short step to not following it at all. So in the first week of teaching a new routine, assume that the child is encountering the activity for the first time and don't stop teaching them. Come back to key routines frequently after the first week and go through the same process. Drip, drip, drip.

In a few weeks you will be initiating routines with the raise of an eyebrow. Other parents will gasp in awe at your skills. They will gently bow as you pass school gates. People will make a path for you in the supermarket queue and stop to congratulate you on your expert parenting.

From the outside, it will look miraculously easy. The truth is always that behind your nonchalant facade, there has been hard work grinding your routines out until they become a family trait. Just another small part of 'How we do it here'.

THE INEVITABLE INFRACTIONS

A friend of mine recalls seeing a father carrying his five-year-old son down the street while the child was repeatedly punching him in the face. The father tried to stem the endless violence with the words, 'Now Jacob, don't do that.' He said it five or six times. The child's punching continued.

A better response would be a firm 'No'. Put the child down and speak to him, holding his hands if he is still keen to punch. All children will test the boundaries. Some will want to test the limits immediately and repeatedly. A small few resent the imposition of order and trample on every rule and routine you can think of.

So it is worth differentiating between small infractions (missing Step 1 of the collaborative homework routine) and more serious breaches (punching Dad repeatedly in the head). You will need to respond differently in each case.

Small infringements need correcting. They need a reminder, maybe a warning: 'Remember our rule about . . .'; 'You need to follow instructions, this is a warning, think carefully about your next step.' These little corrections are simply holding the line, resetting the boundary when it is challenged. There is no need for anger or frustration. After all, you set the rules knowing this would happen. Expect it, plan for it.

Serious breaches of the rules need a more serious response. That escalation should not be in your voice but in your actions. Go to a space where you can speak quietly. Explain the consequences and redraw the boundary (more on both of these shortly); give the child some time to think and reflect. Your response gives them a clear indication that some behaviours are worse than others. We'll explore what to do in each case in Chapter 7.

Rules and routines might feel a bit sterile. But they are the building blocks of great behaviour. The more time you spend teaching them, referring to them and reinforcing them, the more often your child will meet and surpass your expectations.

Without them, 'How we do it here' has no substance, and no real meaning. With them, you can make sure your child knows how to behave in every situation.

TESTING

- Ask your child what the rules are after five days of teaching them. Watch how quickly they recall them and how they are really making sense of them. Compare this to when you first asked them what the rules are and they looked at you blankly and started to guess what might be in your head.

WHAT TO WATCH OUT FOR

- Irritation that your child is throwing your rules back at you. It might be annoying when your five-year-old berates you for breaching the 'Safe' rule when you are perched on the worktop, trying to find the Ferrero Rocher you dropped behind the fridge. It means your rules are working. Now stick to them. Children, like adults, don't like to see the rules not being followed by those in charge. The downfall of many a politician is proof enough.

- Establishing rules and then forgetting to mention them again until someone breaks them. Trying to put out fires by using the rules is not a good idea. Prevention is always best. Mention your rules every day.

- Introducing too many new or revised routines at once. Routine overload just means that you get many routines performed badly, rather than one or two performed brilliantly. Establish your standards early by achieving fewer of a higher quality. Every other routine can then follow.

NUGGETS

- Ask your child to remind you of a routine before you ask them to enact it. Even if this means an extra fifteen seconds before you cross every road for a while.

- Make sure that the rules and routines are accessible, so that other adults in your life can use them too. Write your key rules and routines on a single sheet of A4. Then make it visible to grandparents, babysitters or other members of the family.

- Store your written routines where they are most useful. A small card or Post-it works well. Think about where to put it: the study routine needs to be visible from where studying takes place, the dinner routine is no use if it is just in your head, the respect rule should be prominent on the toilet if you have a boy with a carefree attitude to aiming.

CHAPTER 6

POSITIVE MANTRAS, POWERFUL SCRIPTS

Stop improvising, learn your lines

What you say to your child in difficult moments is a drip-feed of your expectations. It must be consistent. You need to plan it.

What three messages do you want your child to hear whenever things go awry? What if you said the same things to your child in response to their behaviour every day for the next thirty days? What impact would it have on your relationship and their behaviour? I am sure that you would want your words to be affirming, encouraging and positive. These phrases are your positive mantras. They are yours to determine. Drip, drip, drip.

What about the way you bring your child back to the rules? How you react when they step over the boundaries so that you are predictable, clear and calm? You will need to respond to recurrent behaviours in a consistent way and redraw boundaries predictably. These messages are your scripts. Learn them, repeat them. Drip, drip, drip.

These pre-prepared mantras and scripts are the defaults you will return to whenever things get tricky. While positive noticing is about colouring every new morning with uplifting moments, your mantras and scripts are how you consistently respond to your child when behaviour wobbles. They are the bedrock on which you will build love, safety and predictability into every minor correction.

The cumulative effect of sending precisely the same message – day after day, using the same verbal responses – is remarkable. It's another small tweak with a huge payoff. You change what you say to your child, and in turn you change your child's behaviour. You change the norms in your relationship.

DEFICIT LABELLING

We've seen already why language is so important. Tell a child he is naughty and he will internalise it and take it to heart. Tell him he is naughty often enough and he will filter every choice and behaviour through that belief. 'You are always messy'; 'You never sit nicely at the table'; 'You are so rude.'

This principle is even more important when you are correcting behaviour. When you speak to your child in those tricky moments, you need a script. You need to make sure they know you are not criticising their character, just their behaviour.

I learned this from Ruth. At thirteen years old, Ruth was fast losing her way. She would turn up to school because it was something to do, not something to succeed at. Ruth was an Eeyore, albeit a much more aggressive version. Her self-image was as poor as her ability to deal with other people.

It seemed as if nobody had ever told Ruth that she was anything but naughty. This label was attached not just to her behaviour but to her character. She had been told relentlessly that she was naughty by people at home, by her teachers, by her friends and, inevitably, by herself. It became synonymous with her personality. Gradually it became an incurable condition that she could use as an excuse for doing precisely what she wanted. 'Don't blame me, I'm just naughty.'

Trying to praise Ruth was difficult. It didn't fit with her brand. She certainly wouldn't countenance it in public; even one to one she was dubious: 'Yeah right, I don't think so'. Rejecting every positive view of herself and cloaking herself in her deficit label became comfortable for Ruth.

Her grades were less comfortable, though. By Year 8 she was severely struggling at school. The constant negative reinforcement sucked her into a spiral of work avoidance, truancy and school exclusion. She would often be found at the bottom of B block, under the stairs, behind the stack of tables – or 'Ruth's Office' as it soon became known.

The only way to correct this negative self-image was to emphasise that Ruth's behaviour and her character weren't the same: in the minds of the adults and in her own. The central message we landed on was simple: 'I like you, I don't like this behaviour.'

It was a small change in wording. But it was powerful. This deliberate separation allowed Ruth to see that there were aspects of her behaviour that were positive. Her behaviour was something she did rather than something she was. 'Ruth, I like your humour, I don't like food being thrown'; 'I like your excitement, I don't like the shouting'; 'I like how kind you are usually, your behaviour today isn't kind.'

At first, Ruth would reject the statement outright. It was almost as if she wanted us to give up, and it was tempting to think that the strategy wasn't working. But I will always remember the first green shoots. They were visible not in what she said but in what she didn't say. The first time she didn't protest in response to praise. Instead of I'm not kind / I'm not funny / that's not true, she paused. It was the first time that she'd received a positive reflection without a defensive parry.

Changing people's view of themselves is never a quick process. But slowly Ruth began to agree with the positive reflections. Eventually she could see her behaviour as something separate – something that could be managed, changed and improved. It was the first step out of a spiral of negative thoughts. With time, she was able to listen to the positive without reacting. With more time, she was able to listen to it and consider that it might be sincere – even true.

The same principle applies in parenting. Your child and their behaviour are not the same. You need to adopt stock, relational phrases that make that clear, particularly when you are correcting behaviour.

'I didn't like the way that you spoke to me earlier and we need to talk about that now. I love you. Your behaviour is the problem.'

'I love you but we need to change that behaviour.'

'I don't like that decision you made but don't ever think that I don't love you.'

Your child needs to know that your love is not conditional on them making the right choices every time. Nobody can reach that high a bar. They need to know that when there are wobbles in their conduct, you love them regardless.

Tell them. Every time they think they might have gone too far.

POSITIVE MANTRAS

Crafting these positive mantras that make sense to you and to your child will mean that you get the outcomes you need in what were previously moments of tension. Replace your unwelcome factory settings with words that you have chosen yourself. The right words should leap out of your mouth, even if the rest of you may be in panic (or ecstasy) over your child's behaviour.

All that's required is a little planning. You are teaching behaviour and may need to be in teaching mode, in your tone and precision of response. Don't worry. You won't need a clipboard, elbow patches or a casual air of extreme exhaustion.

Crucially, a mantra is not a nag or a moan or an excuse to have a go. 'For God's sake will you please tidy your FRICK-ING bedroom' is not a positive mantra, even though you may have been saying it day after day for many years.

The best positive mantras flow easily into your own speech patterns. They use language that is natural and meaningful to you. They are simple, clear, and not irritating to say or hear.

You might have a mantra that underlines a specific boundary. It can be as simple as 'Remember our rule about . . . '. Deliver it with the same calm and kind tone each time your child approaches an activity that might challenge a boundary.

It always tracks back to the usual rule or routine: the same old line, constantly redrawn.

Or you might want a mantra that reminds everyone of the bigger picture. 'This is how we do it here' works well, obviously. But so do mantras or mottos that pick up on your values as a family: 'Honesty first' or 'Never speak badly to yourself or others' or 'Be humble'. You are reminding everyone of the why factor: *why* behaviour matters and *why* it is part of what you believe as a family.

What is important is that you pick mantras you can stick to. Limit yourself to three at a time. And then get ready to play the long game. Don't expect instant results. You are hoping to change the way that your child thinks about themselves, and that is never a quick fix.

DE-ESCALATION MONOLOGUES

While your mantras should be part of your everyday routine, scripts come in particularly handy in moments of escalating tension. There will be times with children when things spiral dramatically out of control (more on those in Chapter 7). But with the right language you can minimise them.

It is easy to say the wrong thing in tense moments and unintentionally escalate everything. To avoid that happening, you need to work out, precisely, what you are going to say when the chips are down.

The key to de-escalation is saying things that underline boundaries without provoking a defensive response. This script will help with that. When you get the tone, pace and pitch right, it works beautifully. And the better you get at delivering it, the faster it works.

In these moments you are not looking for an instant apology, or even agreement with what you are saying. You are drawing the line, reinforcing the boundary, and letting your child know that their behaviour needs to change. It is one-way traffic, designed not to promote argument but to send a clear, unassailable message. But it is also designed to ensure that the child accepts the consequence with grace and doesn't feel the need to escalate. Everyone's needs are met. Win-win.

1. Connect

Even if you don't feel like it, even if you are still cross, some positive physical assurance is necessary. Your child needs to know that your relationship is still strong, that you still love them despite their recent epic failure. This is just a stretching of the boundaries, it isn't personal. It is a temporary mistake, not a sign of permanent delinquency. If you are about to redraw the boundaries, you need your child to concentrate on that and not for them to be worried about how cross you are.

'As long as you are ok, that is what is important. Come and give me a hug, we can get my phone out of the microwave later.'

2. Notice

Be clear about why you are addressing the behaviour, referring back to the rules. Because you have taken care to notice rather than accuse, you won't encourage a defensive response. This is important because your aim is to get in, deliver the message, and get out – with everyone's dignity intact.

'I have stopped you for a moment because I noticed you have broken our rule about safety. The stairs are not a ski jump, you are not Eddie the Eagle and the saucepan is not an official GB helmet'.

3. Consequence

Tell your child what the consequence is, remembering this doesn't need to be punitive (see Chapter 8). Connect it to the rule-break so that you are clear on why you have intervened.

'I need you to clear all of the cushions and blankets and put them back where they came from/repaint the wall that has been damaged/pay reparations to your injured brother, and then meet me in the kitchen for a chat.'

4. Reframe

As soon as you land the consequence, there is a natural space for the child to protest about it. Quell this immediately by reminding them about a moment when they behaved brilliantly (for younger children, this will need to be something that happened a few minutes ago; for older children it might be earlier in the day or yesterday). This reframing will give them a firm example of how they are already able to behave perfectly.

'Yesterday you played safely outside and made sure nobody got hurt. That is what I need from you again today.'

5. Thank

Thank your child for listening. Keep it short and sweet. And then use the thank you as your cue to leave or change the conversation. Sometimes the monologue can be intense and it is good not to linger. When you get the rhythm right and leave on the right note, it means the child is left feeling clear of the incident and able to get on with their day.

'Thank you for listening.' *[Parent exits, stage left, into the kitchen and out of sight.]*

The more you use this script, the more effective it will become. In a matter of weeks it will be such a part of your routine that you reach for these very words rather than your loudest voice. Your child will expect it and start to predict exactly where the conversation is going. After a month or so it isn't unusual for the child to recognise the start of the monologue and say immediately, 'Alright, I know, sorry, I will clean it up now.' This is useful when you need to draw the line quickly in public. If they repeat your words or learn them and say them ahead of you, don't worry. Just keep to the script.

The script is just a quick underlining of expectations. It is assertive without threatening your relationship; it is kind without any hint of being soft. When you can't think of what to say, reach for it. These words are your backstop when you feel your emotions are too close to the surface. With a well-rehearsed monologue you will start to reduce incidents of unplanned language or disastrous improvisation – freestyles that can turn tricky situations into impossible ones.

Six stock responses to de-escalate any situation

- *'That's not how we do it here.'* To correct small behaviours before they grow.
- *'I understand you feel like that, yet . . .'* To stop the arguing.
- *'You can do better than that.'* To redraw the boundary.
- *'I love you but I don't love that behaviour.'* To separate your child elegantly from the situation.
- *'Be that as it may, those are the rules.'* To manage the answering back.
- *'I need to remind you of our agreement.'* To return your child to the rational plan.

POWER PLAYS

You need a plan – and a script – for every moment of escalatory behaviour. But you need some scripts more desperately than others. Take power plays. A power play is a never-ending argument, often about the tiniest disagreement. Picture the scene:

'I saw you vaping out of the window / eating illicit chocolate / bayoneting Daddy Pig with Henry the Hoover.'
'You didn't see that.'
'Yes I did.'
'NO YOU DIDN'T, you were in the kitchen.'
'No I wasn't.'
'Yes you were!'
'No . . . I . . . wasn't!'

'Yes . . . . . you . . . . . were!'
'I was in the hall!'
'Yeah right!!'
'Yeah!!!'
'I'm not having this conversation! Damn / screw / poo you!!!!'

Power-play arguments escalate quickly. At the end of the battle there are no winners but there is always blood on the carpet. Precisely nothing has been achieved.

So you urgently need a script that can de-escalate the situation. You don't need to force agreement out of a child in order to get the outcome that is best for everyone.

There are a number of simple, consistent scripts that can help here. Partial agreement and a bit of tactical mishearing can be useful. Non sequiturs are your friend. You don't actually have to respond to the nonsense your child is saying in order to effectively de-escalate:

'I did nothing.'
'I know you are a bit shocked by what has happened, let's take a moment.'
'I wasn't even here.'
'It's a real shame but let's get it cleared up first and then we can talk.'
'Bruv, I wasn't even in the country, check my passport.'
'Let's deal with that in a moment, is everyone alright?'

These words help you avoid language that accuses your child. Even when it is obvious what has happened, just focus on the outcome. Nobody likes being accused of something and it sets up a defensive response. The battle then becomes about who is going to stand their ground – rather than what we are going to do about the large curry sauce smear on the cream velour sofa. You need to suppress your frustration, and the stock responses help you to do this. Even if the damaged item is your favourite chaise longue – the one your grandma gave you just before she died – the emotion adds nothing.

The power play is nothing more than a convenient excuse for your child to argue about the semantics rather than the furniture. This is a much more comfortable place for them to be. It is certainly preferable to having to explain why they did a running jump kick while balancing a chicken korma on their head.

ASSERTIVE TONE

As important as the script itself is the delivery. In the same way you rehearse your scripts, you can also rehearse specific tones, words and phrases that have the same effect as the pre-planned monologues.

Let's start with your tone. The extremes of your vocal range might be useful for shouting at the TV or whispering in a library, but they are no use when managing your child's behaviour. Your assertive tone lies somewhere in between. It is controlled and emotionless, firm without being angry.

As you shift into your assertive range, your child will recognise it immediately. They might say, 'Aw, don't use that voice.' That is the right response. It marks a shift from negotiation, which the child might think they have a good chance of winning, to instructions that they need to follow. Even before the language changes, the tone is the first thing to be recognised.

Your child needs to become attuned to your assertive tone. They must know that things have got a little serious. That behaviour needs to be addressed. It shouldn't be unfriendly but should leave aside your usual charm and lightness. There is an intent and a flatness to your voice that means business. It is the tone of the PE teacher with whistle and clipboard, of the call handler who makes you feel a wave of calm in a difficult moment, of someone who knows the rules and is relentless in their pursuit of them. Not aggressive or angry but sure-footed and certain.

The choice of words is also key. All too often correcting behaviour tips over into pleading. There is a desperation to it that shifts your place in the hierarchy. 'Pleeeease don't bully the hamster'; 'Come on, just for me, could you possibly take your finger out of the plug socket?' Nobody responds quickly to this.

Assertive language, on the other hand, implies urgency but never panic. It is more controlled and less emotional than shouting. It means that when things get difficult and have the potential to escalate, your voice remains sure-footed. Try the following language:

'I *need* you to . . .'

'You *should* be . . .'

'When I come back in two minutes, you *will* . . .'

Each term has a subtly different benefit. 'Need' is more insistent than 'I want you to', less begging than 'please could you'. 'Should' works when referring to previous agreements.

'You will' leaves no room for doubt. In each case, the strength is in the language and emphasis, not the volume. In every case, assertive directions work better than pleading.

DRIVE-BYS

Sometimes, of course, saying less is the most effective solution of all. A small nudge towards the right behaviour can be much more productive than a dramatic intervention or hefty punishment. I call these 'Drive-bys': tiny, consistent scripts, delivered positively in passing.

'Do you need some help?'

'Thanks for being ready.'

'Kind voice, please.'

'You are better than that.'

Drive-bys are small moments of coaching that correct, yes, but also encourage and affirm. Little and often works really well. When you circulate the kitchen giving gentle feedback, or pass by the bedroom and correct small behaviours, the atmosphere is set and the boundaries are absolutely clear to everyone.

HAVE I MENTIONED CONSISTENCY?

Consistency in your scripts is key. Even if the child has lost control and your words seem futile against the door slamming and foot-stomping, you need to hold the line. Your consistent scripts will protect you from getting caught in an emotionally fuelled improvisation. When they see that you won't improvise, that you have a plan, they give up trying to negotiate their way out of a consequence. They give up arguing. The perverse 'reward' (watching an adult lose their stack) for behaving badly disappears. Nothing escalates. Everything is calm.

The more this happens, the easier it becomes to de-escalate any given situation. Every time you respond in the same way, your behaviour becomes more predictable and safe.

This repetition matters. Time after time. Tricky situation after tricky situation. If you want to be the parent that every other parent dreams of being, it starts in consistently responding to every challenge.

TESTING

- Practise your monologue on your own or with your partner before delivering it to your child. It is important that you don't fluff it the first time it's actually needed.

WHAT TO WATCH OUT FOR

- Labelling – in particular, deficit labels. Aggressive, annoying, attention-seeking, awkward, badly behaved, challenging, dangerous, threatening, disgraceful, disruptive, feral, malicious, manipulative, naughty, unstable, violent, volatile. These never describe a child accurately. Imagine any of them being applied to you in, say, a performance appraisal at work. We cannot be defined simply by our worst behaviour or unluckiest of circumstances. Faced with such terminology, the expectations become fixed. It becomes difficult to break away from them.

- Conflating your child and their behaviour in your scripts. The message always needs to be: 'I love you, I really don't like this behaviour.' It means the child's character is not under attack. In their own mind it becomes something separate, something that can be dealt with.

NUGGETS

- The first time your child repeats your mantras or consistent scripts, or speaks them ahead of you, don't allow it to irritate you. This is a good sign. It means they have been listening and have started to experiment with the changes in language. Your relational parenting is cutting through.
- There is strength in silence and kindness in a well-timed pause. Sometimes the most positive and relational thing you can say is nothing.
- You can always step out of a power play. You don't have to 'win' anything in the moment. Parenting is a longer game.

CHAPTER 7

WOBBLY MOMENTS

*You don't make children behave better by
making them feel bad about themselves*

Children who reach the limits of their emotional control often engage in deliberately shocking behaviour. They are designed to spin you into a panic: 'What the hell do I do now?'

Don't allow it. In these wobbly moments, your relationship is going to be put to the test. But this is not the time for giving up and walking away. Your child needs you to walk alongside them in the difficult times as well as the good.

These moments will happen. However exemplary you become at positive noticing or de-escalating moments of tension, you are dealing with children. And children can be emotional. In these moments, your response must start with empathy.

Children who regularly lose control of their emotions don't need you to lose control of yours. They need help, not anger. They aren't 'naughty' or 'difficult' or 'trouble'. They are dysregulated and struggling to regain control – and that's a state that nobody really wants to be in.

Sometimes, when you don't know how to say what you feel – or don't have anyone you feel you can say it to – chaotic behaviour is the only way to communicate. Anger is not a confusing emotion and is easy to indulge in, as anyone who has ever shouted knows. Being angry and taking control can feel strangely safe when other emotions that the child doesn't understand are bubbling up.

The last thing you should do is respond in kind. Children don't choose to be dysregulated. Being angry with them is just heaping shame on them when they least deserve or need it. You don't make children feel better by making them feel bad about themselves. Instead, go back to the basics. Keep your emotions in check. Exude calm. Hold the line.

'CALM DOWN'

I once led a behaviour management course with a team of prison officers, who demonstrated how to physically restrain an adult prisoner. They did it with great skill, but the demonstration was performed in silence. I asked if they could repeat the demonstration but this time adding the language they would typically use. I was interested to see how they de-escalated such situations verbally, and how they dealt with the inmates' emotions. This time, they restrained their colleague expertly and took him down to the floor – at which point an officer dropped to his knees and, two inches from the man's face, shouted at full volume, 'CALM DOWN, FUCKING CALM DOWN.'

'Thank you,' I said. 'That was very, um, useful.'

Telling angry adults to 'calm down' isn't helpful. Not because they shouldn't calm down (usually they should), but because it doesn't work. Spoiler alert: it doesn't work with children either. And yet it is a phrase that is deployed almost every time a child is dysregulated.

Dysregulation is an inability to manage your emotional state. It happens. The child might become overwhelmed by the sheer number of emotions coming thick and fast, or the intensity of one emotion that they need help to control. They might find it difficult to soothe themselves and need your help to regulate, whether they are four or fourteen. Dysregulation results in behaviours that might be out of the normal range, and which the child may or may not be in control of.

In these moments, you need a different strategy to the ones we've outlined in the rest of this book. It isn't enough to just remind a child of the rules, or reach for a tried-and-tested de-escalation script. The amygdala is running the show and anything could be on the setlist: running away, slamming doors, breaking things. Alternatively, dysregulation might result in behaviours that are less damaging to the soft furnishings but will inevitably be more damaging to the child. Where adults who are dysregulated might turn to drink or drugs, children can turn to one of the myriad forms of self-harm from unsafe play to hitting themselves to deliberately drawing blood or restricting food. If your child is overwhelmed by emotion, it is important that you tread carefully.

Offer support instead of making demands or threatening to punish. You hear 'calm down' being shouted at children who are beyond the point at which they can regulate their own emotions. In these moments they need much simpler instructions. Calming down can be complicated and might feel unattainable. Losing your temper is exhausting. For children who lose control, it is physically and emotionally draining. The effort needed to regain composure should not be underestimated.

'Calm down' is another of those default phrases. Often, it is accompanied by the adult explaining in intricate detail just how calm they are: 'I am calm, I am sitting here calmly, look at how very calm I am' (usually a lie). There is nothing more infuriating from the child's perspective. It feels as though you are mocking their lack of self-control.

This is not a time for lecturing. It is a time for compassion.

When children are dysregulated, their emotions won't be magicked away with even your most rational argument. I have seen parents respond to tantrums with a series of eminently reasonable points. 'Why are you lying on the floor, it is filthy, think about all of the germs, don't lick it for goodness' sake, have you not seen the research into bacteria on supermarket floors,' etc. Good luck with that.

A child who has lost control of their emotions needs a different approach. They are overwhelmed and their rational thinking is reduced. This is not the time for long conversations. It is not the time to ask searching questions or talk about the 'choices' they are making or bring up the past.

Everything needs to be simple and clear. There will be a time for more detailed conversations when everyone is calm. For now, actions matter more than words.

THE MOST DIFFICULT MOMENTS

I will never forget witnessing a fifteen-year-old girl, Cheris, losing control of herself and of her emotions. It wasn't rational behaviour; her outburst of violence landed on the very people who had spent years working with her. In the space of five minutes she was trying to trash it all: the school, her relationships, her prospects and her ambitions. Sabotaging everything that is positive in your life on the altar of giving over a mobile phone can never be rational. Trauma does this, sometimes.

After the chaos had died down I encountered her leaning against the wall in the hall, clearly still agitated and now lost. I watched as a learning mentor – the lowest-paid member of staff in the school – who had been hurt in the fracas approached her with astonishing skill. He leaned against the wall about three metres from her with perfect nonchalance. There was no threat about him at all, even though he was over six foot and built like a tank. It was clear he had done this before. He dropped his head, looked at his hands and the floor, and just waited patiently. He knew that this was not the time for questions or lengthy conversations. She was clearly overwhelmed and, although she had behaved appallingly, this wasn't the moment to address that.

She knew he was there and turned a little to make sure he couldn't see her face. But she didn't move. That was a good sign. After waiting for the right moment, he said something simple but hugely powerful. 'When you are ready, I am here for you.'

The line was delivered gently but sincerely. He wasn't putting pressure on her or cornering her. Quite the opposite. He was giving her the kindest offer in the most difficult circumstances. She knew in that moment that whatever she did, she wasn't going to be able to push the adults away. It was dawning on her that, even if she had alienated the adults at home, the adults in this school were not going to follow suit.

That message lasts long after you have cleared up a messy argument / incident / full-scale childmaggedon. What you say in the most difficult moments matters more than anything. When your child is most vulnerable, when their emotions are closest to the surface, say little and make your offer the kindest it can be.

EMPATHY FIRST

The goal in these moments is to help the child manage their emotions practically, rather than intellectually rationalise them. When you see your child lying on the supermarket floor, distressed and dysregulated, the intuitive response might be to tell them to stand up immediately. Others might step over them, deliberately ignoring the distress.

The counter-intuitive response – the right response – is to lie on the floor next to them. To make them feel safe again. To show them that you are there for them emotionally, not just there to bark orders. You don't even need to say anything; you are just letting them know that you are there. You are recognising their distress but not trying to take control immediately.

It is going to look a bit strange to passing shoppers for a moment. But the alternative, standing over them and screaming 'Stand up!' over and over, would disrupt them more.

Park the behaviour issue for now. It isn't as important as this moment.

GROUNDING (NOT THAT KIND)

If your child is overwhelmed and struggling to regulate, grounding activities can help. These encourage children to reconnect with the physical world and move away from the overwhelming emotions that are driving their behaviour. They can help your child to slow down the rush of emotion and soothe themselves.

For younger children, this might mean sensory activities – drawing, building Lego, or playing with sand and water. For older children, grounding techniques may need to be more subtle: squeezing and releasing the toes, pushing into the chair with the back/legs/bottom, holding and pressing on a stone/squashy thing, filling the lungs with a big breath, filling a little bit more, then slowly letting the air out through the mouth.

A pre-prepared 'calm box' containing objects and smells that the child knows will help them to reconnect with their calm place. Any box will do. Spend some time helping your child choose objects that could go into the calm box: a small soft toy, a photo of a family member/pet/friend, fluffy scarf, favourite poem, click pen, elastic band for twiddling or squishy ball for squishing. For many people peppermint oil in a small roller bottle works well for panic and anxiety.

This grounding process doesn't have a time limit. For some, it will be relatively quick; for others it might be thirty or forty minutes. Don't try and force it. Be aware that the transition back to unsupervised activity might need to be managed. A gradual withdrawal of support is more likely to smooth this change. 'Right, you have had two minutes with water play and now I want to talk about how rude you were to me' is not going to cut it. It will spin them back into a dysregulated state that will take much longer to recover from.

Five things to say to a distressed child

- *'I am here for you.'* When you can see they don't want to talk.
- *'When you are ready, I am here.'* So that they feel no time pressure.
- *'Do you need a hug?'* To break through the emotion.
- *'Come on, let's walk.'* To relax the conversation.
- *'What can I do to help?'* When they seem stuck.

SECONDARY BEHAVIOURS AND HOW TO IGNORE THEM

When things have calmed down a bit and your child's emotions and actions seem more regulated, you will want to address the behaviour itself.

But this isn't always straightforward – when you try to address the original behaviour, it may quickly morph into others. Perversely, these new behaviours might appear to be nothing to do with the original incident. Welcome to the wonderful world of secondary behaviours.

Secondary behaviours are those that come after the behaviour you are trying to deal with has stopped. They can throw you off balance. Take Maureen. For a seven-year-old, Maureen was highly skilled in the art of exasperating adults.

Having the name Maureen in the twenty-first century was a trial; as a result, she had developed some advanced defensive skills.

Skill 1: smirking. According to the basic laws of human behaviour, children are not supposed to smirk.* Nobody likes a smirk. Maureen had worked this out. Whatever the occasion, Maureen would respond to being corrected by smirking. It started off as a nervous response. But over time she learned its power.

A well-deployed smirk at the right moment can enrage an adult whose focus was, until then, simply on the telling off. Almost immediately, attention is diverted from the original crime. The conversation quickly focuses on the smirking and allows Maureen off the hook. Rather than talking about her rudeness or why she was carving her name in the table with a toy car, everyone suddenly moves to the smirking conversation.

It always started the same way – 'Take that smirk off your face' – and developed in a similar vein – 'If you don't take that smirk off your face' – before escalating into – 'How dare you smirk at me like that' – and eventually – 'Go to your room.'

All this was safe, predictable ground for Maureen. From her perspective, a raised voice or two was worth suffering if it meant she could behave with impunity and then be banished to her favourite place. It was incredible how many adults she seemed to have control over – and how many times sustained smirking got her out of a sticky situation.

* I am sadly not clear on what said basic rules are for adults.

Maureen's behaviour is a classic move in the aftermath of a wobbly moment. In these moments, secondary behaviours are common. Think of them as 'chase me' behaviours, designed to skilfully distract you from the original incident. They might even be worse than the original behaviour.

This seems irrational: why is my child escalating things, even after the original behaviour seems to have stopped? It may not make sense to you, but then the child might be driven by emotion not reason. In their attempts to avoid consequences for the primary behaviour, they escalate things, sometimes quickly.

There are all sorts of secondary behaviours. Smirking, of course. But also turning away, eye-rolling, slamming doors, hiding in bed, breaking things, damaging possessions, walking/running/sprinting out of the room, blaming someone else. And, of course, swearing, because it works every time. If you want to distract someone from your poor (primary) behaviour, there is nothing better than the well-deployed (secondary) profanity. The stronger the better.

Whether it's conscious or not, the child's goal is always the same: distraction. And as with Maureen, the consequences follow a similar pattern. It is easy to get trapped in a cycle of 'up-sanctioning' – in which both you and your child escalate and escalate, and you get further and further from the behaviour you were originally discussing. The child takes control of the situation. And the punishments increase as fast as you can come up with them. 'Look, there is no need to swear, I just wanted to talk to you about . . . You are shouting. *Right!* No screen-time today . . . Why are you ripping that up? *Right!* No screen time for a week . . . Where are you going?

Right! No screens ever again . . . Why are you packing a bag, whose taxi is that?'

This is a cycle of exponentially growing reactions. Very soon, you run out of consequences and find yourself surrounded by chaos. You need to find a way to de-escalate things.

However counter-intuitive it feels, put aside the secondary behaviours for now. Focus only on the primary ones. Even when the most provocative secondaries appear on the scene, don't change tack. Insist that the original behaviour is addressed.

If that isn't working, take a break and walk away. When you come back, return to the original behaviour. You don't need to win every battle straight away.

Four ways to deal with secondary behaviours

- *Recognise them for what they are.* A distraction from the job at hand.
- *Gently bring the conversation back to the behaviour you came to deal with.* 'I came to talk to you about how the spade ended up through the neighbour's conservatory window.'
- *Keep an eye on your emotions.* Don't allow the secondary behaviours to provoke your emotional response.
- *Save it for later.* Which is when you can talk about the secondary behaviours calmly: 'When we spoke earlier, you kept interrupting/turning your back on me/telling me I am a "wasteman".'

FOGGING

How do you bring the child back to the conversation that you want to have about the primary behaviour? As the adult, you probably want to get to this point as succinctly as possible – to go from A to B without deviation. Alas, this isn't the child's plan; if they can interrupt your A to B with F, Y or Q, they know that there is much to be gained.

Sometimes, when the child is an expert diverter, you might forget the original conversation altogether. Their tangents are often deliberate, learned behaviours designed to get them off the hook. In these moments, fogging is your friend. This refers to a gentle, calming fog being cast over the child's protestations. It's not meant to confuse (but maybe to gently dampen). It stops the child from taking you off on a tangent and keeps you focused on the behaviour in question.

This is another counter-intuitive. Fogging works because, even in a defensive argument, it says to the child, 'I am listening.' Often when children argue, the instinct is to stop them in their tracks: 'I'm not listening'; 'I'm not interested', 'I don't care.' These methods are risky because, believe it or not, they allow your child to walk away thinking that you don't listen, you aren't interested, and you don't care.

So rather than shutting them down, use a simple sentence stem that gives the child the opposite impression: that you do care, but that this time it is going to go your way. It does not mean that you are changing your response or that you are encouraging a negotiation. It simply means that you hear them. Try these:

'I understand . . .' (works with all levels of complaint)

'You might be right . . .' (doesn't commit you to any
    change of direction)

'I hear you . . .' (children know they are heard, even when
    you're not going to follow their line)

'Be that as it may . . .' (compellingly meaningless – and
    yet accepting of the child's view)

Each of these sentence stems could be followed with a 'but'.
Instead, try the gentler and less abrupt 'And yet . . .' to loop
back to your expectations. You can now fog skilfully and empa-
thetically, every time de-escalating the situation and bringing
the child back to the primary behaviour that needs addressing:

'No way am I doing that, get lost.'
'I understand how you feel. And yet our agreement is . . .'

. . . with seeming acceptance of a different view . . .

'But she was doing the same thing and you haven't said any-
    thing to her.'
'You might be right. And yet what we need to do is . . .'

. . . or perhaps more directly . . .

'I'm sooooooo bored of this shit.'
'I hear you. And yet our rule is . . .'

Make sure you are talking about 'we' and 'our' at this stage,
not 'you'. When tensions are high, you must stand alongside

your child, not over them. This small gesture makes a big difference. You are no longer in accusation mode but in solution mode.

Above all, fogging works because it is empathetic. You can acknowledge your child's protestations, appear completely reasonable, and then continue with the conversation you were having. When you get it right you will be able to bat away their complaints and tantalising distractions, and get your message across with the outcome you need.

When you leave the conversation, you will leave your relationship intact. There is no trail of anger and resentment left in your wake. Your child feels listened to and that they've had a chance to speak. You'll walk away from what previously would have been conversational carnage with a skip in your step. The addictive kick of great parenting.

NOTICING WITHOUT ACCUSING

It's not just the child who can derail your interventions in wobbly moments. All too often, attempts to deal with bad behaviour turn into a barrage of accusations: 'It was you who painted the walls/stole the chocolate biscuits/put cat litter in the dishwasher.' Alas, anyone who finds themselves being accused instantly becomes a barrister for the defence. A small observation about behaviour can quickly escalate into a lengthy courtroom drama.

Again, your choice of language holds the solution. One of the gentlest and least judgemental ways to address poor behaviour is to start with a mere observation: 'I notice'. There is always an opportunity to notice instead of accuse. 'I notice you are halfway through the cat flap'; 'I notice you are hanging off the guttering'; 'I notice you are drinking the ketchup from the bottle.'

'I notice' makes a potentially tricky intervention an exercise in studied nonchalance. There is no shame or blame attached to 'I notice'. As a result, it is one of the quickest and easiest wins. Don't emphasise it, throw it away. Be casual with your 'I've noticed' moments and you will find yourself having more conversations about behaviour and less arguments because of it.

Noticing is also helpful after the fact, when the wobbly moment has ended. 'I've noticed you haven't had any homework for a few days'; 'I've noticed you are hanging out with Sam again'; 'I've noticed your PE kit is still in your bag.' Use it every single time you intervene with poor behaviour, before or afterwards.

THE ILLUSION OF COMPROMISE

With the help of lots of fogging and even more noticing, you will find the wobbly moments become less fraught (and less frequent). Nevertheless, there are times when compromise – or at least the illusion of compromise – is wise.

Sometimes, you will feel that your conversation with your child is becoming stuck in a loop of refusal. Consider a classic of the genre:

'I want to go and play some more'

'It is bedtime'
'Play more'
'Bedtime'
'Play'
'BED!'

Deal-making is a great way to help your child out of these spirals of refusal. It is often just a reframing of expectations using the word 'Deal'. To the child it feels like a deal; in reality, it is just a way out for everyone. It gives the child a get-out and makes them feel like they have some agency. It gives you a chance to stop chasing absolutes ('BED!') and means that the moment won't be spoiled with tears.

There is a trick to such deal-making, however. It's easy to give too much ground. When you make a deal with your child it does not mean that you renegotiate the rules. Nor does it mean that you won't get the outcomes you want. You get to structure the deal, and if you get that right it will *feel* like a relational concession to the child. It can help everyone find another way during an argument that is going nowhere.

This deal-making starts with a simple offer. Instead of the accelerating frustration, try 'Can we make a deal?' or 'I can do a deal for you if you are interested.' Then make a deal that sounds enticing and offers your child a way out of their persistent refusal to follow instructions. Make sure there is no concession or bending of the rules. 'If you go to bed now and follow our ready rule, then I will make sure that I give you more warning tomorrow night before you need to stop playing. Deal?'

Children are highly likely to accept a deal when it is offered. Even if they haven't listened to you properly, if there is a deal on offer then why not say yes. You are, of course, offering nothing dramatically different to what you would usually do.

Just make sure that you are not offering anything that would mean the rules are changed, even temporarily. You are a skilful negotiator, holding the line while appearing utterly fair, reasonable and kind. It is such skilful parenting that you would get a BAFTA, if you only had a camera crew to hand.

RECOVERY

However wobbly the wobbly incident, there will be a point at which it appears to be over. This is a delicate moment.

The psychologist Lenore Walker once developed a model called 'The Aggression Cycle'. She pointed out that well after somebody seems to be in recovery, there can be an 'explosion phase' that arrives once everything seems calm. It is at this stage that there is most risk of reigniting the child's emotions.

So it is important that you give recovery time. That might be ten minutes. It might be an hour. Be aware that if the child becomes agitated or upset or enraged straight away, their next outburst is likely to be even more exaggerated. Recovery is fragile and it is easy to find yourself back in the original argument at an even higher volume very quickly.

Plan so that this explosion doesn't happen. Take care with what you say and the way you say it. Now is not the time to pick through the bones of what has just happened to see who is to blame. It is not a time to make demands or insist on an apology. Take a break, have a walk and a drink, talk about something else. Take time to recover properly and slowly.

Difficult conversations might need to be had later. But for now the priority is recovery.

TESTING

- Try saying less. When you find yourself in a difficult situation in which behaviour is dysregulated and possibly extreme, just don't speak or do as much. The intensity of the moment might not need your fury or emotion or control. It might instead be improved by your pause, silence and ability to gently step back.

WHAT TO WATCH OUT FOR

- Allowing other people's views on what you 'should do' to influence you. People often try to help or offer advice, particularly when you are out in public. They may have the very best of intentions but they don't know you or your child or what has gone before.

NUGGETS

- Don't rise to 'I hate you'. It is a phrase designed to inflict maximum damage on a parent: the one thing you never want to hear. Yet some children will use it repeatedly to try and retaliate. I know it is difficult, but don't react to it. And never, ever throw it back at them. You don't need to play tit for tat.

- The miracle of the present infinitive tense. Sometimes it's best to simply observe what you see: 'You are standing on the table'; 'You are swinging from the branch'; 'You have muddy shoes on the carpet.' Simple observations spoken aloud can force the child to immediately reflect on what they are doing rather than try to defend their choices.

- Kindness every time. When you are stumped by the behaviour, when you don't know what to do next, when nothing seems to work, kindness is always the best response.

CHAPTER 8

PROPORTIONATE CONSEQUENCES

The ferocity of the punishment doesn't determine future behaviour, but it might determine your future relationship

The Punishment Road is littered with terrifying sanctions. Parents get seduced by the idea that you provoke behavioural change through a winding path of ever-increasing punishments, each designed to persuade the traveller to turn back, mend their ways and never pass here again.

At the end of the Punishment Road are consequences whose harshness and ugliness defies comprehension. The idea is that at some point the child will have a 'road to Damascus' experience and suddenly realise they must take a different path.

The angrier the adult gets, the faster the child is pushed down the Punishment Road. Often steps are jumped due to a sudden fit of rage: 'For God's sake, I have told you three times to stop doing that. I'm removing your pocket money for twelve months!'

Some children see the Punishment Road and, quite sensibly, don't want anything to do with it. They don't need harsh punishment or even a mild rebuke. They are self-correcting. I am guessing that if this is your child, then you are reading this book for voyeuristic pleasure only. I mean, you are welcome nonetheless. I don't mind.

A few children, on the other hand, seem to skip down the Punishment Road, accepting every consequence with a perverse eagerness to see where it goes. Each punishment is a small, necessary sacrifice to find out what is at the end of the road. These are precisely the children that the terrors of the Punishment Road were designed to intimidate. And yet they couldn't care less. They aren't fazed by any form of punishment and will accept them all gladly.

Some children follow the rules, some follow people. If you try to force a child who follows people to follow the rules, you will go mad. For these children there is no punishment so gruesome that it will make them change their ways. A different approach is needed.

If this is your child, you already know about it. You will have tried escalating punishments, lengthy sanctions and the harshest consequences. They will all have impacted more on your relationship with your child than on your child's behaviour.

If this is the case, you need to rethink your approach to consequences. From time to time all children need to be reminded of where the line is. But it is not, ultimately, the size and frequency of the punishment that determines future behaviour. If it was, this would be easy. We would all reach for the largest consequence, apply it repeatedly and behaviour would be changed forever.

It doesn't work like that. It never has.

TOUGH LOVE AND TONNES OF BRICKS

Many parents justify taking a hardcore approach to punishment with a simple phrase: tough love. But where tough love is always tough, it is rarely love. Being hard on your child to teach them the lessons of life isn't a good plan for parenting.

Tough love is the result of unreflective, intuitive parenting. Rarely is it planned; instead, it is usually the consequence of a rush of emotion in the adult. Conversation is rarely part of the picture. Neither is reasoning. To the child, this doesn't feel like love at all. Children don't call it tough love. Only adults do.

In these cases, the punishment is assumed to teach the lesson. It doesn't. I once worked with a headteacher who was waging a forever-war on bad behaviour. 'We have tried everything,' he told me. 'We have detentions every lunchtime and after school every day. We have recently started holding lengthy detentions on a Saturday morning. We are doing all that we can: behaviour just isn't improving.' So what was his next plan, I gently enquired? 'Well, that's obvious, Paul,' he told me. '*Sunday* morning detentions!'

As this headteacher learned, the fact that even the heaviest penalties don't work can be deeply frustrating. 'Stamping down on bad behaviour' is a favourite of every parent who feels they haven't been strict enough.* Of course, coming down on children like a tonne of bricks is a shock-and-awe tactic. It won't work, and won't improve anything in the long term, even if it might make you feel better for a while.

* See also: every politician who wants more votes.

The Punishment Road is festooned with these ineffective, punitive sanctions. In a blur of disciplinarian irrationality, parents find themselves declaring the most ridiculous sanctions. It is only with time to reflect that they realise they may have been a little hasty in banning their child from 'THE INTERNET. FOREVER!' – considering they rely on it for schoolwork and in almost every other aspect of their lives. A similar effect is caused by parents who use lengthy grounding as a punishment. After the first week of their child not leaving the home, they are frustrated by the empty fridge, child-shaped dent in the sofa and the teenage takeover of the lounge, now replete with large piles of half-eaten snacks.

The only real effect is to divide the adults and children into 'them' and 'us'. It creates barriers within the family, encouraging your child to be more deceptive to make sure they get caught less often. It is easy to take things away; to teach 'No'. It is much harder to teach 'Yes', and to encourage and reinforce new behaviours in the process.

EMOTIONAL PUNISHMENTS

These overwrought consequences aren't the worst element of the Punishment Road. In an attempt to curb the most undesirable behaviour, many parents use emotional punishments.

Using emotional pain to uphold boundaries is a brutal and unhappy way to parent. One classic strategy is to take away from the child what they most love, an approach that will certainly cause immediate and often lasting emotional upset. I have heard teachers at parents' evenings ask about this while searching for a sanction that might work: 'What is it that she really loves that we could take away?'

But this is an intuitive response, not a rational one. Taking away access to their favourite sport, friend, place or hobby risks attacking what they value most. Why attack the thing in their life that is going really well; the place where they feel most positive, confident and powerful? Consequences in the adult world are never this harsh.

At the very end of the Punishment Road lies physical punishment. You might not be surprised to hear that physical punishment is going to damage the relationship between you and your child instantaneously. But this is true not only of smacking, but of the more low-level physical consequences you might mete out in anger.

The frustrated yank of a young child's arm might not be intended as a physical rebuke, but to the child it feels like one. Pulling them out of bed by the ankle might assuage your annoyance, but to the child it seems like a physical consequence. Even waving your arms about in front of your child's face is very close to connecting physically. So set yourself a rule that you won't ever put your hands on your child in anger. Don't allow it to happen, even by accident.

These disproportionate punishments aren't just ineffective. They can erode the relationship between you and your child. The size and ferocity of punishment doesn't determine future behaviour. But it might just determine your future relationship.

THE KIDDY POLICE

Disproportionate punishments come in many shapes and sizes. Some misguided but understandable, some outright bizarre.

The bizarrest, perhaps, is the frequent invocation of the authoritarian might of the State. Parents often use the police as a backstop to support their (often strange) parenting choices. Most of the time, threats to summon the police are not a response to extreme behaviours, but simply to a build-up of small, irritating ones. From 'I'm going to call that policewoman over if you don't stop avoiding the cracks in the pavement' to 'If I have to call the police because you won't eat your peas, they will lock you up.'

This willingness to invoke the criminal justice system can reach extraordinary heights. Like the invention of the Kiddy Police.

The Kiddy Police first arrived after a few nights in which my friend's four-year-old, Alice, had refused to go to bed at the agreed time. Each night, a different sanction had been threatened; each night, Alice was still awake past 10 o'clock. The presence of older children on their summer holidays certainly wasn't helping matters. Like many of us, Alice didn't want to go to bed as she feared missing out on the fun that was bound to happen.

The Kiddy Police seemed to be the solution. It was introduced quite casually one evening: 'Oh yes, the Kiddy Police come round every night at 7 pm to check that children are asleep in bed.' The concept was easily explained and instantly accepted by Alice.

This was an odd invention, but not one that at first caused any huge anxiety. (The thought of the police knocking on doors at 7 pm might be a little out of place in a liberal democracy, but Alice didn't seem to notice.) However, the second part of the Kiddy Police's responsibilities was more terrifying: 'If they knock on the door and find that you aren't in bed, they turn you into an adult and take your childhood away.'

This is quite a dramatic escalation of events just to try and convince your child that they need to go to bed. It's funny, granted, but it's no joke to a four-year-old. At the same time, you are buck-passing – on this occasion, not even to a co-parent, but to an imaginary demi-god.

It is an understandable instinct. Like the all-consuming terror of the Christmas Elf checking his list, some parents want their children to believe there is an all-seeing eye watching their every movement. This is not a sensible way to ensure good conduct. Convincing your child that they are under constant surveillance doesn't scream mutual trust. One might argue that it is how your child behaves when you aren't around that tells you how well you have taught them.

The final risk comes at the point when the child realises that they have been misled by the parent; when the Kiddy Police, Behaviour Fairies, Kindness Leprechauns etc. are revealed as a ruse. Suddenly all the authority that was ceded to the higher power vanishes and the parent must try and re-establish themselves as the person in charge. That is a difficult and unnecessary transition just as the child is waking up to the world outside the family.

We have long lists of imaginary characters that bring joy to children. There is no room at the inn for ugly characters with dubious motives. The buck stops with you. Let your child know that in terms of their behaviour they are answerable to you, and there is no higher power ready to swoop in and save them.*

3-2-1 CONSEQUENCE

Not all disproportionate punishments are as weirdly creative as the Kiddy Police. A more common alternative is '3-2-1 consequence'. You know the one: 'If you don't stop doing that by the time I get to zero, I'm going to [insert deranged punishment here].' The idea is that a quick countdown from three gives the child enough time to realise that what they are doing is wrong, stop mid-flow and immediately change their behaviour.

3-2-1 is ubiquitous. Notice it when you are next in the supermarket or at the school gates. The range of consequences goes from '3-2-1: right, no toy' to '3-2-1: right, we are going home and never coming out again' to '3-2-1: right, I am leaving you here and you will have to live out the rest of your days in aisle 9 of Morrisons between the pasta sauce and ramen noodles'. The levels of anger on display by the adult range from mildly irritated to full Vesuvius.

So many parents use this method that you would think it was a scientifically proven technique; that years of research

---

*Kiddy Police update: after telling my friend that she would end up in my parenting book, I had a video message from her daughter thanking me sincerely for 'stopping the Kiddy Police from coming round'. This is magnificent. Now when there is something she doesn't like, she asks, 'Will Paul put this in the bin like he put the Kiddy Policy in the bin?' I have become the Kiddy Police, police. (With thanks to Dr Charlotte Taylor for the story.)

and gathering evidence had produced the perfect antidote to children not following instructions. Unfortunately, nothing could be further from the truth. There is no reliable research or trustworthy guru demonstrating that 3-2-1 is a good idea. (And if you find one, tell them to come and see me.) It's an urban parenting myth.

3-2-1 fails because it takes the place of conversation, reminders, warnings and proportionality. It is one-way traffic coming at speed. It has no positive encouragement, no reference to rules or agreements, no collaboration. It is instead designed to put the child under extreme time pressure. Often the 3-2-1 is uttered so quickly that the punishment is being dished out before the numbers have left the adult's mouth.

If there is no immediate response from the child in terms of a change in behaviour within the countdown, the adult assumes all punishment is deserved, even welcomed. The child's failure to comply is interpreted as an attempt to be deliberately insolent. Suddenly, the full buffet of punitive punishments are available, and the parent imagines they have earned the right to select a particularly juicy one. They have said the magic numbers, after all.

You see the absurdity of '3-2-1' when you imagine using it to manage adults. Have you considered trying it on a friend or your partner? I ask this because I don't think you would be brave enough to try it. I am guessing that the reaction would not be entirely positive and possibly violent. I can't see anyone complying with instructions without considerable protest. It wouldn't improve your relationship (or your sex life). It would probably be brought up and ridiculed at every opportunity in the future.

It doesn't work with children either. Young children tend to cry immediately – a reaction not to the consequence but to the speed and ferocity of the countdown. It is too hurried and induces panic, not rational thought. Older children often simply ignore or shift into defensive mode at the perceived humiliation. It is hard to change the way you feel for the better instantaneously. If your child is behaving poorly out of anger or frustration or upset, then expecting them to snap out of it is unrealistic. Adults can't do that and they might have had a lifetime of emotional development.

Your child is emotionally immature by design. Expecting them to surpass the expectations for an adult is unfair.

Instead of out-loud declamations of 3-2-1, internalise it. Use it for your own emotional control. And use the opportunity to think carefully about the next steps. Once you've calmed down, instead of threatening a terrible punishment, take your child back to the rules: 'Remember our rule about . . . ?' Remind them 'how we do it here'. Stand alongside them for a quiet word or run through the agreed routine again together. Use it as an opportunity to teach.

There are always more than three seconds at your disposal. There are so many ways to coach and adjust behaviour that are more effective and don't rely on sudden admonishment.

THE NAUGHTY STEP

A relative of the 3-2-1 punishment is its mutant cousin, the 'Naughty Step'. Now don't get me wrong. The Naughty Step is an improvement on shouting at your child, but that is a very low bar.

You can see the appeal of the step. Sometimes children do need to be asked to leave a situation. So it is useful to have a place to go. The trouble is, there's often a second function of the step: humiliation. It might be on public display. It might even be decorated with the words 'Naughty Step'. Christ.

Soon, the Naughty Step becomes a place where children are expected to sort out their emotions on their own. It's a place they go to self-regulate. But children who struggle to regulate their emotions are not better left alone. They need 'time in' with an adult not 'time out'. Forcing children to regulate their emotions alone when they haven't been taught how is just cruel.

You can't expect children, particularly younger ones, to redraw their boundaries for themselves. They need an adult to help ground them, regulate with them and to walk alongside them. None of that happens on the Naughty Step.

TOXIC SHAME

'3-2-1 consequence' and the Naughty Step both depend on shame to work, particularly when used in public. They are supposed to change behaviour by encouraging the child to feel at best privately embarrassed, at worst publicly humiliated. But shame is not a good teacher. It teaches terrible lessons; ones that you wouldn't want your child to learn.

Shame-based punishments are ubiquitous. For years, shame was viewed as an acceptable way to manage and curb a child's behaviour: standing in the corner wearing a Dunce's hat at school, etc. While this might seem like another world, shame still forms a huge part of modern parenting. From public shouting to private disappointment, from 'you're an embarrassment' to 'you have let everyone down', shame is everywhere.

Yet punishing with shame is not a proportionate response from an adult; it is an emotional barb that sticks, painfully.

Your relationship with your child depends on mutual trust. And nothing erodes trust like using shame as a tool for managing behaviour. It is always a disproportionate action. It is the fastest way to drain your emotional currency account and risks driving a wedge between you and your child. Your relationship will suffer.

People remember being shamed for a long time. When experienced as a child, shame can damage self-esteem, self-image and self-belief. Just talk to anyone about their worst subject at school and a faded wound will quickly reappear in their adult life.

So be aware of it. Weed it out. Reflect on what you say to your child and how it leaves them feeling.

This might be easier said than done. Many parents make no deliberate use of shame. It is just another default. If your own childhood was full of shame-based punishments, it is hardly surprising that it is having an influence over your parenting choices today. It creeps in, unnoticed, through the unthinking use of emotive language. 'It's a pity you can't . . . '; 'Are you proud of yourself?'; 'You are selfish/hopeless/careless/no good'; and the classic: 'You should be ashamed of yourself.' Then there are labels that encourage blame alongside the shaming: 'attention-seeking', 'aggressive', 'malicious', 'manipulative', 'feral'. All this language makes the child feel inadequate, whether by accident or by design.

The context in which you talk to your child can also induce shame. Calling out someone's behaviour in front of others rarely ends well. When there's an audience, the stakes are raised. Defensive responses are guaranteed as a result. Giving your child a loud talking-to in the swimming pool changing rooms might relieve your Saturday morning frustration ('Why can't you put your own socks on? You are three. It is about time you grew up!'). But it won't encourage your child to enthusiastically pick up their armbands the next Thursday.

DESERVES VS NEEDS

None of this means that you shouldn't use consequences, or that every consequence should be a cup of squash and a hug. There is a balance to strike.

The key is proportionality. There's a simple question you need to ask yourself over and over: What response to this behaviour is going to get the future behaviour I want?

In order to answer that question, you need to focus not on what feels intuitively right, but on the desired outcome. You can give a child what they 'deserve' for their poor behaviour. Or you can give them what they 'need' to actually change it. The former approach results in tariffs and hierarchies and a childhood rich in random and scarring punishment. Done badly, the latter can feel like the child 'has got away with it'. But done well, it can have real, lasting effects.

Imagine a large gauge with a needle. On one side of the gauge is what the child 'needs'. That will include what they need in the moment and also what they need to learn better behaviour. On the other side of the gauge is what the child 'deserves', which can often be an irrational (but gratifying) response from the parent.

Ask yourself where the needle points on your Needs v Deserves gauge. Do you lean too heavily towards 'Deserves'? Perhaps you find yourself issuing countless punishments that don't seem to have the desired effect? Or worry that in retrospect your punishments were too harsh? Or find yourself having repetitive conversations about consequences which invariably cover the same ground?

If so, you need to gently nudge your pointer further towards 'Needs'. At this end of the gauge, your goal is to use the smallest consequence that will be effective. Don't reach for the worst sanction on the shelf. Reach for the one that will deliver.

THE SMALLEST CONSEQUENCE THAT WORKS

The goal, above all, is to avoid punitive consequences. 'Sit there for a minute' is not punitive; 'Sit there for an hour' is. 'Go to your room and I will come and speak to you' is not punitive; 'Go to bed without dinner' is. 'I am taking the toy away for now' is not punitive; 'I have lobbed your toy out of the eighth-floor window' is.

Punitive consequences seek to 'drive the message home', but what they actually do is damage trust. So instead, you need to impart the lesson that is required, nothing more. What you are looking for is the smallest consequence that is effective.

If you go in with large sanctions you won't just appear unreasonable, you will have left yourself no headroom. If things deteriorate you will have nowhere left to go: 'Right, well now I am going to double it. You are never leaving the house again, TWICE!'

There are lots of options for proportionate consequences that positively teach better behaviour, rather than ones that simply teach 'No'. Here are a few to consider.

Rational Consequences

A rational consequence is calm and logical. If your child sprays paint all over the kitchen, then having a five-minute chat about it might seem to the child like a great deal – a bargain, even. So don't be surprised if there is a repeat of the 'indoor paintball' saga tomorrow. The rational consequence is that they need to clean up the mess they have made. If they are too young to do it themselves, then they need to help you clean up the mess. Making good, repairing and mending can all be appropriate rational consequences. The key is fitting the right consequence to the child, the context and the situation.

Agreed Consequences

You might want to agree on some consequences that you will use in advance so that they aren't a surprise to your child when they appear. Perhaps resist listing every possible consequence your warped mind can muster and instead focus on just three. Outlining them in advance will reduce the likelihood that you will resort to disproportionate consequences because you are feeling angry/upset/like emigrating alone. Just as you shouldn't freestyle tricky conversations, you shouldn't freestyle consequences.

Practical Pay-Back Consequences

Look for consequences that ensure the child is paying back into the family. You may not be able to reclaim the cash value of the illicit ice cream stolen in the middle of the night, but there are other ways to pay back: doing more chores, helping with dinner, washing up. Remember, though, that some pay-back consequences are more trouble than they are worth. 'You are doing all of the laundry for the next month!' sounds great. However, a bit of forethought would save you the agony of having to watch a nine-year-old throwing washing chaotically into the machine on the hot cycle and seeing the whole family clad in comically shrunken woollens for the next six months.

Immediate Consequences

The consequence is always better when it happens close to the incident. Younger children in particular need a consequence that is immediate and applied as soon after the incident as possible. Put lunch, a TV show and a trip to the swimming pool in between action and consequence and the consequence becomes meaningless. For very young children, put any activity in between action and consequence and you have ruined the lesson: they have forgotten what you're talking about. A teenager can deal with more delay, but dishing out consequences next week or next month will mean they are similarly pointless. You might remember turning up at a school detention with no idea why you had got it, only finding out weeks later that it was your history teacher from a lesson a month ago.*

Five small consequences that work

- *Going to bed ten minutes early.* As a consequence for getting up late.
- *Having to listen to Radio 4/Barry Manilow/War and Peace in the car.* As a consequence of poor behaviour on the road.
- *Delay of privileges.* Rather than taking them away altogether.
- *Reduction in screen time.* Rather than throwing the Xbox in the bin.
- *Removing them from an event for a pause.* Rather than banning them from the event for its entirety.

APPLYING CONSEQUENCES WITHOUT THE DRAMA

Deciding on what the consequences are isn't enough. You also need to plan how to apply them. Without the drama.

* No? Just me then?

By now, you will not be surprised to hear that consistency is key. Think through how to deliver a consequence in the wake of different behaviours well before they happen, and what consequences you might consider reasonable in the cold light of day. Improvising punishment – and letting your emotions decide on your behaviour – must quickly become a thing of the past.

You might want to structure your responses in a few steps. This helps children understand that there are recurrent consequences for repeating poor conduct. Perhaps more importantly, it also helps you to maintain perspective by having a well-thought-through plan. Without clear steps it is easy to go from small consequence to huge punishment in a heartbeat. For consequences to be effective they must start small, then rise logically in the smallest steps possible.

These steps help you to keep calm and resist the 'This is the 17th/34th/472nd time I have told you' approach. They might also help you to see the behaviour for what it really is – a child testing the boundaries rather than a child seeking to wind you up. The steps are not a solution in themselves; just because you get to Step 4 doesn't mean that the behaviour will magically cease forever. But they are an effective, reusable measure to help to teach new behaviours.

1. Reminder

'That isn't a nice thing to say. Remember our rule about respect. This is your reminder.'

The final phrase is important. You want this request to stand out among all the general daily reminding. Your

repeated use of this phrase means the child will start to recognise it immediately. It will become a signal to everyone that
behaviour needs to change.

2. Warning

'You have chosen to use that language again. Being kind is
important. This is a warning.'

Again, the final phrase is key. It is firm, a bit formal and
more insistent. It gives the child notice that you are going
to take action if boundaries are not respected. There is no
huge escalation from reminder to warning, but the shift in
language and tone tells its own tale. The warning stage is the
last opportunity the child has to change their behaviour and
take control of what happens next. Beyond this point you get
to decide what happens. You will take control.

3. Time-in

'Let's take some time-in, and step away from people so we
can talk about this properly.'

Time-in is so much more effective than time-out. Time-
in means being with an adult, whereas time-out relies on the
child self-regulating alone. Time-in with an adult means a
conversation and a space to regroup. Older children who have
been taught how to regulate might need some time alone,
but there is still an opportunity for conversation and recon-
necting with an adult. If the behaviour is extreme, you may
need to move to this step immediately; but for smaller trans-
gressions, only ever build up to 'time-in'. At this stage you get

to decide what happens – and what, if any, consequence is proportionate.

4. Consequence

'You will now need to go to bed ten minutes early this evening. Do you remember yesterday when you shared your toys brilliantly, that is what I want to see from you now.'

If you do need to apply a consequence that is more serious than a reminder, a warning or some time-in – and you won't always – then frame it in relation to your child's previous good behaviour. You are reminding them that this is a deviation from the norm, not who they are. (You are also reducing the chances of a small-scale riot.)

BEHAVIOUR AS COMMUNICATION

All behaviour is an invitation for you to respond. If you respond to behaviour with instant anger and punishment, you are either ignoring or missing what is being communicated. Meanwhile, the need for the child to communicate will not go away.

Punishment might quell the outward behaviour for the time being, but you will find yourself in a messier situation later, when your child recommunicates it louder and more clearly. Possibly in a way that you cannot ignore.

So when you are delivering consequences, think not just about the desired outcome, but what caused the behaviour in the first place. What was your child attempting to communicate, however clumsily? What are the signs that you could learn for next time? And how can you support them when it happens again?

This isn't a search for blame or an attempt to heap guilt on already guilt-ridden parents. It is a method to learn, refine and improve your responses for next time. There is always a way that we can adjust our own behaviour, if only we dare to reflect.

TESTING

- Allow some time (particularly the first time). After you deliver a consequence it is important that your child has the chance to correct their behaviour. It is tempting to stand over them and watch to see if they are going to comply immediately. This is not an atmosphere in which good decisions are made. Walk away, turn your back, let them decide to either follow your instructions or not. Give them a little time to decide what they are going to do.

WHAT TO WATCH OUT FOR

- Raking over incidents in forensic detail. This is never a good idea. It inevitably brings up the same argument that you have just spent ten minutes trying to stop. So keep things really simple. Don't go over what just happened. Apply the consequence gently, remind them of the boundary, remind them of better behaviour, and move on. Trying to search for blame or unravel a 'he said'/'she said' spiral is a waste of time.

- Making reasonable consequences unreasonable. Small reasonable consequences repeated too often soon become irrational. 'You will need to go to bed five minutes earlier for every time you have been rude to me. Your current bedtime is 11 am.'

NUGGETS

- A proportionate consequence is weighted with the heft of the action, not the heft of your emotion. It at once says 'No' and also seeks to teach better behaviour.
- Before you intervene, separate. Remind yourself (and your child) that they and their behaviour are not the same. Which is fortunate. It is easier to work on the behaviour than to try and change your child's character.
- Practise viewing behaviour incidents as teachable moments. They are golden opportunities, even if they don't feel like it. Use them well.

CHAPTER 9

RESTORATIVE REPAIR

*Punishments don't teach better behaviour,
restorative conversations do*

The world is full of people who believe that their behaviour doesn't affect other people as much as other people's behaviour affects them.

We all meet this attitude in our own communities. Sometimes we can see it in the mirror. But if we are striving to create a society in which people look out for each other, then children need to learn the impact of their behaviour on others.

The question is how. In the last chapter, we learned what proportionate consequences to wrong behaviour look like. In the end, though, punishment is not a great teacher. Done wrong, it is scattergun, random and often disproportionate. But even done right, it won't fundamentally transform how a child behaves. For that, you need them to self-reflect and to make a plan for similar scenarios in the future. You need a restorative conversation.

When tempers have frayed, when manners have disappeared, or when things have been said that should not have been said, restorative conversations are the only way to meet everyone's needs. Unlike punishments, they offer a plan to deal not just with the incident itself but with the restoration and repair afterwards.

That means that the long-term answer to improving behaviour lies in the structured, planned conversations you have with your child. Once again, it is not available as a quick fix. Once again, work is needed. And once again, that is mostly going to come from you.

Sometimes, parents are brilliant in a crisis. They deal with the most difficult behaviours in the moment. But then they don't follow up. They might be so exhausted by the behaviour that they don't have the energy for the repair. Perhaps they don't want to risk inflaming the situation again.

Either way, without the restorative conversation, nothing is learned beyond 'you have broken the rules'. It is less than half a job done. You need to teach your child how to reflect on their behaviour and create a plan for the future.

RESTORATIVE CONVERSATIONS

A restorative conversation is not a restorative justice conference. Such conferences take place over days, as victims and perpetrators of a crime come together, discuss what happened and find ways to move forward together. They are detailed, painstaking and conducted at a pace that allows everyone time and space to engage. If you hold a restorative justice conference every time your child called you a poo-poo head (insert age-appropriate equivalent here) your whole life would be spent in conference.

Restorative conversations are shorter, and structured around up to five questions each time. They are over in minutes, not days. And they are simple enough to be used in a wide variety of situations. It is nothing more than a parenting conversation with a bit more planning and structure; one that helps everyone to walk through incidents logically, redraw the boundaries and do some thinking about future behaviour.

The defining characteristic of a restorative conversation is that it seeks to repair damage. When trust has been broken or relationships have been harmed, they come to your aid. Sometimes they will replace punishment, sometimes they will run alongside other consequences. Restorative conversations are important, however, as their focus is on understanding and learning.

Small things matter when repairing a relationship. In terms of the restorative conversation, often it is the adult who gets to make all the decisions: what the questions will be, the order in which they'll be discussed, where the conversation takes place, how long it is and when it starts and finishes. This is not always the best approach. I am not suggesting that you give all these choices over to a six-year-old. But it is worth reflecting on the power imbalance so you can adjust things a little. You must demonstrate to your child that they have a voice; that this is a conversation in which their opinion matters. This means that the outcome should not be predetermined, and that you give your child some say in where, when and for how long the conversation takes place.

Above all, it means you entertain the possibility that as well as them being accountable, you might need to be too. Sometimes we all have a 2/10 day and, on reflection, realise we could have behaved better. Styling it out and pretending you did nothing wrong is exactly the wrong model for your child. Be honest. Answer the questions truthfully and with humility, just as you wish your child to.

Most of the time you will be blameless. But nobody is blameless all the time.

APOLOGISING, FAST AND SLOW

For this reason, a restorative conversation cannot simply be a prelude to the child apologising. If it is framed in this way, then it is simply a one-sided conversation with only one outcome. The child knows that there is no real search for truth or mutual understanding. They know that whatever they say, whatever mistakes the adult may have made, the result is them performing a gracious apology. Is it any wonder that parenting chats often begin with the child saying: 'I'm sorry. Now can I go and murder some people on the computer?' They would rather skip the interrogation and get back to the cyber-murdering.

Don't get me wrong. Children (and adults for that matter) should apologise when they are at fault. Just not as an automated part of the process. There is no sincerity in that.

There are many ways to apologise. There are some days when an apology doesn't come easy and needs to be returned to later or the following day. Functional apologies rely on children simply going through the motions – they hold no real meaning and are just the performance of rehearsed lines. Often, an apology will be the right outcome. It cannot, however, become routine. It needs to arrive organically, the result of a restorative conversation.

At the same time, a restorative conversation is not a negotiation. It is not an opportunity to blame the adult, or for the child to try and excuse their behaviour. There is no question about your authority. There may well be times when you reflect on an incident and decide that your own behaviour didn't really help. But the restorative conversation is not designed to pick apart what you've done. It is a chance for the child to look in the mirror, to view their own behaviour and see their choices reflected back at them. It is a chance to see if there are different ways to do things in the future – and a chance to consider who else might have been affected as a result.

CONVERSATIONS THAT WORK

The end goal of every restorative conversation is for the child to think about the effects of their actions on others.

I once worked with a teacher (now a brilliant head-teacher), David Lisowski, in the early days of introducing restorative conversations to schools. He was convinced that there was real power in this sort of conversation and offered to 'have a chat' with children who had been removed from class.

This was a large, inner-city comprehensive with all the challenges that came with it. It was not a place that had previously entertained a restorative approach to behaviour. But within a few weeks, David was having restorative conversations with children from multiple classes, and adults could see that they were having an effect.

With the permission of the children and their parents, he sent me video footage of children answering questions and reflecting on their behaviour. One of these involved a twelve-year-old boy, Kai. 'Who has been affected by your actions?' David asked him. Kai replied with a very definite: 'Me. Just me.'

At first, Kai couldn't imagine that he had caused anyone else any difficulty at all. So David patiently explained to him that his outburst in the classroom had indeed caused difficulties for a number of people. He calmy and logically explained to Kai who those people were and how they had been affected, 'When you threw the book across the room and it hit Fay in the face, she was affected. Mr Knight was affected as he had to stop teaching, something that he loves more than anything. Miss Ali was affected as she had to come and remove you from the room. And I have been affected as I have left a student who needs help to talk to you. Don't forget, of course, that Mum will be affected as I am going to have to call her at lunchtime and talk through what has happened, and I know she doesn't like being called at work.'

Kai listened carefully, eyes widening. This was a complete revelation. The idea that his behaviour could affect others detrimentally seemed to upturn his whole view of the world. David questioned him to check that he understood: 'So Kai, can you just remind me of who has been affected today?' And Kai repeated to David what he had been told: 'Fay, Mr Knight, Mrs Ali, you, Mum and me'. As he did so, the realisation of the effect of his behaviour was written across his face.

'That's a lot of people, isn't it, Kai?' David said. Kai nodded, with genuine regret. A solemn, thoughtful nod, monumentally reflective for a twelve-year-old who is usually lost in his own world.

In that moment, David demonstrated why restorative conversations are the only route to long-term behaviour change. You don't get that kind of learning from punitive punishment. You only get it from leading a child to think for themself.

THE RESTORATIVE FIVE

How to conduct these conversations, then? It's easy to overcomplicate things. A restorative conversation isn't a police interview featuring a tape and legal representation. Keep it simple. Five questions is enough; for younger children, two.

I have given you more than five questions here, so that you can choose the most appropriate for the situation and for the child. You won't need them all. You'll know the conversation is over because you'll have talked through the incident, viewed it from a variety of different perspectives and made a plan for what happens next. Most of the time your restorative conversations will be simple and resolve perfectly. Sometimes things can be a bit messy, and the conversation reveals more information that changes the outcome.

Get comfortable with the restorative conversation being a conversation, rather than an instant solution to all your problems. As you address each of your questions together, remember that in between your truth and their truth is *the* truth. The questions are for the child but also for the adult. Even if it is clear from the outset that the adult is not at fault, you still need to answer the questions; not because you must always account for your behaviour, but rather because your model is essential. This must be a two-way conversation, not an interview.

1. What happened?

Listen carefully and dispassionately to the child's account of what happened without interrupting or disagreeing. Then they need to listen to your account too, without judgement.

Memory is a strange beast. Recalling what happened so that both parties know exactly the behaviour that is under the spotlight is a vital starting point. Steer clear of 'and then *you* decided it would be clever to empty the paint on the guinea pig'. Take care with how you present your account. Go slowly and step carefully. After all, if you have already decided exactly what happened and decided on the outcome of the meeting, then all of this questioning is redundant.

At the same time, you mustn't let the conversation devolve into a forensic examination of the punishing detail of what happened. When an adult and a child try to recount the fine detail of the same incident, memory lets everyone down. What is remembered – language, context, poignant moments – is recalled with different emphasis and emotion. So your goal is to establish the basic facts and move on.

2. What were you thinking at the time?

This question helps the child to reconsider their actions and replay their thought processes. It encourages self-reflection.

Their thinking at the time may have seemed irrational to you – possibly, in hindsight, to them also. However, it may not be obvious to the child that their initial behaviour was misjudged. It is worth spending a little time trying to see the events unfold from their perspective.

Your own perspective is also a vital element of this. Your judgement may have been skewed by other distractions, and you may need to reconsider your own response. Self-reflection is not just for children. How you viewed the incident at the time may have been influenced by a huge range of factors, including your mood, other people watching, tiredness, and even the time of day. It is always healthy to review judgements that you made in the cold light of day.

3. What have you thought since?

Even if not much time has passed since the incident, both of you will have reflected on it. This may have given the child an opportunity to step back, change their attitude or shift their explanation. And it would have given you the opportunity to do the same.

The answers to this question will vary depending on when you choose to speak. Your conversation needs to take place when everyone is calm. Immediately after an incident is not a good idea, particularly if everyone is still feeling upset by it. But there is no hard and fast rule; when you decide to speak is a judgement that you need to make for your child. The younger the child, the closer to the event the restorative conversation needs to be. For older children you might wait an hour or so, or perhaps until the end of the day.

4. Who has been affected and how?

The child might be completely unaware that their behaviour has affected anyone else – younger children, in particular. Often the response to 'Who has been affected?' is 'Me, I have been affected, I am sitting here talking to you when I should be playing with my friends online, it was my game that got broken and I am the one who is not able to play it anymore.' It is only after some gentle encouragement that the child is able to see the bigger picture. 'When you threw the console across the room, Granny got hit in the eye, so she was affected. I have been affected as I should have started work five minutes ago. Your friend has been affected as she is waiting for you to go and play . . .'

You will find that the more you unwrap this question, the easier it becomes for the child to answer it. You are teaching empathy, directly and successfully. In time, these reflective questions might even pop into their head before they act. You are encouraging them to use their awareness of others to drive their behavioural choices.

It isn't enough just to recognise that others may be affected. To encourage a deeper empathy, explore *how* they have been affected. How did it make them feel, how was their day changed, what might they be thinking about what happened? At the end, ask the child to list again the people who have been affected, perhaps underlining the point: 'That is quite a lot of people who have been affected, isn't it?'

5. What should we do to put things right?

There are many possible answers to this question. Of course, there is an apology. But there might also be cleaning up the mess, repairing a relationship, doing a good deed, writing a letter – and perhaps most importantly, changing behaviour. This is a great moment to teach values: what we should do to put things right, but also *why* we should put things right.

The child might need help in finding the right options; they might need a nudge in the right direction to find an answer that fits. The answer to these questions is never the same from one conversation to the next.

6. How can we do things differently in the future?

This is the moment at which the boundaries are redrawn. It is when future behaviour is modelled. This doesn't mean that things will go perfectly next time, but it means there is a good chance it will be considerably better.

It is also the point in the conversation at which standard responses are more likely. It is clear that the conversation is nearly over, and it won't be the first time your child has felt like they need to promise the earth to stop the talking. Rather than encouraging a response that is full of undeliverable promises, drill down into the detail. 'When I ask you why you are late in, instead of telling me to "shut up fam", just say "sorry Mummy" and give me a hug.' You will naturally help your child rethink some of the decisions they make. They may well have already thought about this and use you as a sounding board. It is a good note on which to finish the restorative conversation.

The worst thing you can do at the end of the conversation is to give a summary of your judgement. 'Right, so now you admit you were wrong, and say you are going to apologise, and never will you be horribly rude to the postman again.' This is the opposite of the point. A restorative conversation hasn't been designed to lead to any judgement, at least not of others. At the end of the conversation, tell your child that you love them, have a hug, and move on.

The last memory of an event is often the one that lasts longest. You want your child to look back on the restorative conversation knowing that it was fair, calm and reflective.

Four more restorative questions (to swap in and out)

- *What was unusual about today?* For when you think the context affected the behaviour adversely.
- *Why do you think things went wrong?* An open-ended question for older children who are good at reflecting on their actions.
- *Where do we go from here?* For the times you feel your child is able to resolve things themselves.
- *Who could help us with the next steps?* For when you or your child needs a bit more support.

GETTING THE MEETING RIGHT

Restorative conversations are simple but not easy. You need to plan everything: the setting, the moment, the atmosphere. The more you plan, the more likely you are to change behaviour in the long run.

Start with the basics: your own emotions. However irritated you are with the behaviour that provoked the conversation, try to focus on the outcome that is best for everyone. That means going back to first principles: emotional control from the adult. Trying to have a restorative conversation while you are still fuming is only going to end up making things worse. Above all, don't bring punitive consequences into this meeting: neither the threat of them, nor a discussion about what they might be this time or next time. It will taint the discussion and mean that it is never truly restorative.

You also need to find the right environment. Restorative conversations are much more straightforward when they are one to one. Don't be tempted to hold a restorative conversation with more than one child. Trying to do this with two children at the same time means they don't just see their own reflection in the mirror, they see their sibling's reflection too. This doesn't afford any space for self-reflection. It simply risks sparking conflict between siblings during the discussion.

This principle applies to parents, too. If you are co-parenting, resist the temptation to have two adults and one child involved. It doesn't feel fair to the child that there are two of you. It will change the atmosphere and conversation and will stifle their voice. Very often the adults will be trying to manage each other as well as the conversation, and this shifts the focus entirely. Even if you assume that you are perfectly aligned as parents, this is not the time to publicly test that out. Send your partner off to make the tea instead.

Next, the setting. Restorative conversations should never be conducted like an interview, with the two of you facing each other across a table. This isn't an interrogation, so turn off the spotlight and stop pacing. Instead, try doing something active while you talk. Walk and talk, play with playdough while you talk, build monsters with Lego while you talk, go for a drive and talk. The distraction of doing something that doesn't require constant eye contact frees the conversation up. It takes the pressure off the child to come up with instant answers. It becomes a less attritional conversation and a more reflective one.

This conversation isn't about establishing your authority. It is about creating a space in which your child can speak without fear.

Getting the setting right also means picking your moment. The meeting must be given the time – and therefore the importance – that it deserves. It can't be squeezed into a couple of minutes before bed, or be a quick chat before school. Plan for ten minutes at a time, when running over won't be a problem. You don't need to take up all the time; a good restorative conversation can take half that. But what nobody needs is the pressure of time when the sole focus ought to be on repair.

Finally, plan for what comes after the meeting. How are you going to end on a positive note? How will you bring things neatly to a conclusion so that everyone can move on? Resist the temptation to tag something else on at the end of the meeting: 'Oh, and before we finish you were also rude to . . . '

Once it's over, don't be tempted to mention the meeting or agreements that you made in front of siblings or your partner. Don't allude to it or use it to embarrass or correct. You will undermine the trust needed and find that subsequent meetings have a different tone altogether. For restorative conversations, standard Vegas rules apply: what happens in the meeting, stays in the meeting.

This means that private and sometimes sensitive conversations feel genuinely safe. This safety matters. A good restorative conversation is nurturing, and the process of repair critical in promoting behaviour change. You are walking alongside your child during the difficult miles. It is so much better than 'Oh leave it, he'll get over it' can ever be.

WHEN CONVERSATIONS GO WRONG

Benke was highly intelligent, wonderfully literate and appallingly behaved. The sort of child who would spend the entire lesson messing about, doing absolutely nothing, or applying full make-up/nails/pedicure – only to present immaculate work at the end. It was quite remarkable.

Her behaviour didn't appear to be damaging her own education, but she was certainly damaging others'. So it was that I found myself having a few restorative conversations with Benke. One to one she was delightful. She would give the most eloquent and apt responses to the questions each time; she would make all the right noises, punctuated with the requisite sorrowful eyes, and promise earnestly that 'the best apology is changed behaviour'. I started thinking that I should apply for some 'Teacher of the Year' award. These were the restorative conversations you dream of. Naturally, nothing in her behaviour changed at all.

Expecting every meeting to have the desired effect simply because you are calm, kind and well planned is unrealistic. Benke had become a master at the art of the restorative conversation in all the wrong ways. She was not genuinely looking in the metaphorical mirror (ironic, as she spent most lessons looking in a real one).

Restorative conversations take time to have an impact on some children. Some will deliberately sabotage them just to see if you are going to persist. They might find the mirror that is being held up difficult to look into. You could get one-word answers to your carefully selected questions. They might try to divert the conversation. They might just cry and not want to talk at all. Or they might, like Benke, just be really good at deflecting.

In Benke's case, I eventually started mixing it up a little. Instead of sitting down to talk, we walked and talked. Instead of the same predictable five questions, I used others without warning. I challenged any stock responses that she offered and dwelled for longer on 'How can we make things right?' Her answers became less planned and more honest. She was forced to reflect more and deflect less. Slowly, her behaviour in a class of thirty became closer to her behaviour on a one to one. Small changes were effecting a big change in the child. Bingo. Now, where did I put that 'Teacher of the Year' application form?

My experience with Benke made me realise the importance of flexibility. The questions you ask, the moment you
speak, the tone you adopt – all need to be carefully chosen on
a case-to-case basis. If your child clams up and is finding the
conversation difficult, you might choose to pause and resume
in a few minutes. You could also try nudging them with some
different perspectives.

1. Thought experiments: 'Ok, I know that you don't
   think that people have been affected, but imagine if
   there were, who might they be?'; 'I know it is difficult
   to know how to put things right sometimes. What
   could the choices be?'

2. 1 to 10 scales: 'On a scale of 1 to 10, how frustrated
   were you when I stopped you?'; 'On a scale of 1 to 10,
   how cross were you feeling?'; 'On a scale of 1 to 10,
   how badly have others been affected?'

3. Choices and nudges: 'Do you think that picking some
   flowers would help?'; 'Can we write her a note?';
   'Would you like me to be there when you speak
   to her?'

Remember that some children find these conversations
easier than others. The reflective state of mind takes practice. Some people are naturally more reflective thinkers. They
are able to see their own behaviour for what it is, think hard
about it and work out for themselves the changes that they
need to make. The rest of us need help with that. The more
we practise, the better we get.

NEW DAY, CLEAN SHEET

Incidents colour everything until they are resolved. If you wait until the next day to have your restorative conversation, it will hang over everything in between. So aim to deal with things promptly, and definitely before bedtime, so the new day is untainted by what happened yesterday.

It is important that your child knows that every day is an opportunity to reset their behaviour and start afresh. Otherwise, conversations and consequences seem to be never-ending and hang over them across weeks and months. That is an uneasy feeling. It doesn't take long before the child feels that they can do nothing right. The bad stuff never leaves.

When things happen late at night, it isn't always possible to resolve things there and then. So in rare circumstances you might deal with any outstanding issues before or over break-fast. As they finish their food, a positive day is now possible. New day, clean sheet.

If your child is in a pattern of poor behaviour, it is even more critical that you adopt this mantra. It is easy for them to feel as though consequences are piling up. Wipe the slate clean every day and start the day with some positive noticing. Even – especially – if you think the day is going to be as bad as the one before. Without a clean sheet, it is easy for the child to give up on the day before it has started. After a few days of repeating the same mistakes, their expectations of themselves will be at rock bottom.

Your own expectations might also have plummeted. But it is your high expectations that will shift their behaviour for the better. Like Eliza Doolittle, the flower girl who wants to be a

lady, it is your expectations that drive the change: 'The difference between a lady and a flower girl is not how she behaves,
but how she is treated.' You have the power to influence the
day for the better, every day.

With a clean sheet, expectations can be reset each morning
and remain high. Remind your child that every day marks a
new beginning. That every morning is a new positive moment.

RESTORATIVE PARENTING

I have had the pleasure of leading hundreds of restorative
conversations with children of all ages, backgrounds, races,
nationalities, shapes, sizes. I have had conversations that
provoked tears and rage. Conversations that needed to be
stopped because they weren't going well. And conversations
that couldn't be stopped because the child was so into it.

I have learned to wait and then wait some more for
answers; not to prompt too quickly; and not to be scared of
long silences, because at the end of a long silence is often a
golden nugget. A good restorative conversation includes the
full voice of the child, not just a mumbling agreement at
the end of each question. This takes time to develop. Don't
expect it first time round.

I have had children who have turned King's evidence before
I have even got the first question out: 'I done it, you got me
banged to rights, proper, take me down to the cells and throw
away the key . . .' And others who say as little as possible until
the very end, when they realise that there is no huge punishment waiting to drop. Then they want to talk for hours.

Some trust the conversation and format straight away; some are more suspicious. It may take time before they realise that the questions are not part of an elaborate set-up or a search for blame. But when children finally learn to trust the process, it is a revelation.

A restorative culture in the home is about more than just using structured conversations to repair damage. It requires a willingness to resolve behaviour in a logical, rational way. It means that decisions on behaviour happen when things are calm, and not in the heat of a crisis.

Holding repair and restoration as key principles affects every conversation about behaviour. The underlying assumption is that problems can always be resolved without drama. That children have agency and a voice in finding solutions. That adults can be trusted to lead fairly and kindly. Homes with a restorative heart are calmer, there are fewer blow-ups, and there seems no need for stand-up rows.

Building a culture around restoration rather than punishment is tough. It is the harder path, where moments of learning replace hours of penitence. But the results are transformative. A restorative culture beats the Punishment Road on ethics and, most importantly, on outcomes. It is the only way to create behaviour change that lasts.

TESTING

- Limit yourself to one restorative conversation a week for the first few weeks. You don't want overload.

Track the outcomes and monitor the behaviour of your child subsequently. What ideas did they hold on to? Which behaviours crept back in? How long did that take? How has your relationship shifted? What effects have consequences/positive recognition had since?

WHAT TO WATCH OUT FOR

- Too much repetition. For some children, hearing the same questions each time provides a consistency that they appreciate. For others, the repetition encourages game-playing. They quickly learn which answers work best in response to which questions. They learn to answer to please you, and there is no genuine reflection. They are no longer looking in the mirror. In this case, you need to change the questions around, mix them up and reduce the ability of your child to just go through the motions.

- Excessive power imbalances. Remember that from the child's perspective there is a serious and perpetual power imbalance in the relationship. Adults have all the power, the control and the money. You can't eradicate this completely, but you can recognise it and take steps to minimise it. How you organise your restorative chats, the tone you use, and who gets to make the decisions can help provide some balance.

NUGGETS

- Ask yourself the questions too. It is a dialogue, not a shaming session. Your model is everything. Your ability to be reflective and analytical will be picked up on and imitated.
- Not every restorative conversation will be a triumph. If the meeting is a disaster, if your child cannot manage a respectful conversation, just pause the meeting or postpone it until a better moment.
- Don't call them restorative conversations. Or your child will know you have read a book about it. They are just conversations.

THE PARENTING PLEDGE

A target is just a wish until it is written down

Humans are fickle. The reason many parenting strategies fail is the difficulty of committing to them in the long term. It is common to hear 'Tried it, didn't work' or 'He's still the same as yesterday' or even 'Nothing seems to work with that child.'

But behaviour takes a long time to change. Embedding that change properly takes even longer.

It is easy to set off with the best of intentions and then get distracted. Before you know it, four days have passed since your last bout of positive noticing or the invocation of a positive mantra. But tell me it doesn't work after a month, not after a day. Change will take longer than you expect. It will be worth it.

So make a commitment to change how you parent. Write it down. A target is just a wish until it is written down.

Start by focusing on the week ahead. Write down your pledge for the one change you will make in the next seven days. Attach it to something that you will see every day: the back of your phone, the dashboard, your keyring. Or go and find a pebble that represents your promise and put it somewhere obvious, with the note tucked underneath. Every day that you see the note or pebble or keepsake will reaffirm your commitment to the task. It will remind you why you are doing this.

Then be ready to renew it. A seven-day promise soon becomes a month of repeating the mantra; within two months it is just part of 'How we do it here'. It works, I promise. I have seen adults who made seven-day promises and five years later still have the pledge on their keyring – a little reminder of where they started. Parents don't change in one dramatic transformation. Small changes done properly over time have the most impact.

THE PARENTING HARE

The Parenting Hare reads a book on parenting, and before they have even turned the last page have put every idea into practice.

The Parenting Hare picks up ideas and runs with them at full speed until exhaustion.

The Parenting Hare's home has routines emblazoned on the walls in neon lights, posters declaring the new rules, and a mood room set up for restorative conversations before breakfast (formerly the lounge).

The enthusiasm for new ways of working is admirable, the passion remarkable. But the Hare's plan is chaotic, rushed and bound to fail. Strategies implemented in a hurry are always implemented badly. As each new initiative piles on top of the last, the true value of the ideas becomes lost in the chaos.

Changes cannot be made all at once or secured within a few days. You can change the way that you parent immediately. But your child will take a little time. This is a marathon, not a sprint. Little and often is the key. Slow and steady wins the race.

To improve behaviour, it is Tortoise Parenting that triumphs. Each incremental step means that the mood is calmer, boundaries are tighter, the relationship stronger. You will feel things getting better and staying better. Changes made at a pace that suits your child mean you won't need to stop to rest. The relentless, slow, drip, drip, drip of positive change is critical.

That first seven-day plan, then, is a tiny plan. Simply choose one thing to work on for a week and write it down. One idea to try out, one small change to test. If you try to do everything in this book at once it will be initiative overload, you will burn out very quickly and your child will think you have had a personality transplant.* Instead, you could spend a couple of months working on your emotional response and another couple just on positive noticing. Do each one once and do it right. Make sure that the changes are secure and embedded before you move on. Make sure the changes have become your defaults before you think about adding more.

As you introduce each tiny plan, look out for the effect it is having. Throughout the week, make a point of remembering

* Or perhaps read a parenting book.

when your child's behaviour shifted simply in response to small changes. Perhaps they escalated things to see if they could get the same reaction. Or tried to ignore positive reflections until they were irresistible. Don't expect miracles, simply observe the power of your influence. Try to recognise each time you change your own behaviour and the effect it has on you both.

Make the changes subtly. There is no need for a fanfare or a big 'Let's talk about your behaviour' meeting – or worse still, 'I've read this book and it says . . . '. Just keep at it. Habits are formed through repetition. Don't worry about how you are going to keep up this new approach for the rest of your life. Think only about the next week. Hopefully my voice will be somewhere in your head, encouraging, positively noticing and occasionally saying, 'Oi tortoise, slow down!'

Five tiny plans for a Parenting Tortoise

- *A week without shouting.* Not even to get your children to come to dinner.
- *Positive noticing three things.* Every morning before school, if you can.
- *Resolving to use 'I've noticed . . .'* Each time you correct behaviour.
- *Refusing to chase secondary behaviours.* Always return instead to the original.
- *Sustaining an unshockable poker face.* Even and especially when things are escalating.

YOUR NINE-STEP PARENTING PLAN

Each time you introduce a change, commit to it properly before you move on to the next one. Give yourself time. Set yourself realistic targets and be prepared to move them if you can't meet them. Everyone's situation is different. There can be no hard deadlines.

The nine steps that follow are how this all breaks down. The order of the steps is important. Start at Step 1 and work your way through at your own pace and in your own time. Don't skip to Step 2 because it seems a bit easier, or jump steps as you think you have nailed it in forty-eight hours. If it takes you six months to conquer your emotional control, well, that is time well spent.

Step 1: Emotional control

- Decide that you won't react to the next incident with a screwed-up face, a raised voice or by rolling your eyes. Being unshockable in the face of poor behaviour will mean your child gets a very different response. Celebrate your excellent parenting every time you hold to that decision.
- Disconnect their behaviour from your emotion. All that matters is the link between their behaviour, the rules and the consequences. Keep your emotion out of it in the moment, even if you allow yourself a scream or two in private.

Step 2: Consistency

- Write down a list of 'How we do it here' right now, before any changes have been made. Think about how you deal with poor behaviour right now, how you celebrate their over-and-above behaviour, and what your current expectations are. Now write down the changes you would like to make and draw up a list for the future. Share it with your child, post it on the fridge and return to it every day in the first few weeks.
- Think about your own consistent model. Constantly come back to an internal question: 'What would the best parent in the world do right now?' If you like to eat Coco Pops in your pants, enjoy road rage incidents, swear at the neighbours or lie in until 1 pm and smoke Camel filterless, I understand. But not when your child is around. They need a better model.

Step 3: Positive noticing

- Make yourself a positive noticing tally. Aim for at least ten positive noticing moments a day. Keep it subtle. There's no need for party poppers or to announce great news about your child's behaviour to the other customers in the supermarket.
- Each time you positively notice, reference 'How we do it here'. 'I love how you shared those chips, that is a great example of how we do it here.' And question for understanding: 'Why do you think that behaviour is so brilliant?'

Step 4: Teaching new behaviour

- Bin the behaviour games. Work out what your default methods are and see if you can go a week without using them, whether that's phrases, token economies or crime sheets. If you fall off the wagon, get straight back on. None of us is a perfect role model. The key is to try every day. To work on it rather than ignore it or pretend it has no impact.
- Start growing new behaviours with attention, praise and love. Assume that your child is going to behave well and do the right thing. Shift your language so that that assumption is implicit: 'Thank you for . . .'; 'I know that you will . . .'

Step 5: Rules and routines

- Decide on and communicate your three rules. Sit down with your child and discuss each one in turn, noting down useful ideas. 'How would these rules be followed when we are out? When you come back from school? When I am not here?'
- Establish and teach one three-step routine. Talk your child through your expectations. Each time you start the activity in the next week, take a moment to check your child can recall the routine and its sequence.
- Start to include the rules and routines in instructions. 'We need to tidy up. Can you think which rule/routine would be helpful to think about before we start?'

Let everyone who looks after your child know the rules and routines that you use. Ask them to reinforce them positively and sincerely.

Step 6: Mantras and scripts

- Start using assertive sentence stems to correct behaviour. 'I need you to . . . '; 'I've noticed'; 'When I come back I will see . . .' every time you address poor behaviour.
- Don't be afraid of being repetitive. Seek out the bits of script that work for you and then hammer them home. 'I love you but I don't like this behaviour'; 'This is how we do it here'; 'Remember when you did this brilliantly.'

Step 7: Wobbly moments

- Check yourself each time you criticise your child's character rather than their behaviour. Notice yourself doing it. If necessary, apologise and retract it. Keep your child's behaviour and their character separate. There is a world of difference between 'I don't like you' and 'I don't like that behaviour'; between 'You are crazy' and 'That behaviour is crazy.'
- Practise fogging. Use the key sentence starters 'I understand . . . '; 'I hear you . . . '; 'Be that as it may . . .' when your child tries to argue or distract you from their behaviour or the consequences.

Step 8: Proportionate consequences

- Plan your response to poor behaviour so that you can deliver consequences without drama. Know exactly what your consequences will be beforehand so that they are predictable, proportionate and fair.
- Reflect on the smallest consequence that works in your home. Give your child less of what they 'deserve' and much more of what they 'need' to behave better. Deliberately resist consequences that rely on shame, silence and 'tough love'.

Step 9: Restorative conversations

- Start with one restorative conversation this week. Make it a good one. Hold up a mirror to behaviour and teach how to manage similar situations in future.
- In the days before your conversation, use single restorative questions as part of gentle enquiry into your child's decision-making. It means that your child will get used to thinking reflectively and be used to the questions when they are weaved together in a restorative chat. 'What could you have done differently there?'; 'Who might be affected if you did that?'; 'We need to put this right, how could we do that?'

Eventually, you will have covered everything in this book. At every turn, remember the focus: not them, you. Your own behaviour is the central cog that turns all others. When you get that right, all the little ones around you will soon be whir-ring smoothly.

TESTING

- At the end of the first day of no shouting or positive noticing, think about how the last twenty-four hours have gone. Has anything changed? What reactions did you notice from your child? How do you feel? Has it been the first day of being the best parent in the world? Good. Now keep going.

WHAT TO WATCH OUT FOR

- Setting fantasy outcomes that you can't possibly achieve. They set everyone up to fail. 'Perfectly impec-cable behaviour in every situation' within two weeks might be a little unrealistic for a child who is strug-gling to follow even basic instructions.
- Making your targets your child's problem. Take care not to transmit your anxiety to them: 'Look we only have a week to get this bit right.' Your time pressure should not become theirs.
- Giving up too soon. Some children will need more time to shift their routines and expectations. Set your-self some small, realistic targets so that when you have a bad day and think that you are back to square one, you can recognise how far you have come.

NUGGETS

- Write down a snapshot of where you are now, before you make any changes. This will be an important peg to return to if you ever feel that nothing is making a difference. Write it as a set of bullet points, a one-page summary, even as a story – but make sure you keep it safe, so you can remember where you once were with your child's behaviour.
- Celebrate the small changes. It needn't be in public. But find a way to congratulate yourself for achieving little milestones. Positive noticing works for adults too, even if you have to do it for yourself.

LAST WORD

Everyone responds well to a calm approach. Children pick up on it straight away and the response is real. Your calmness is contagious.

As the shifts you have made in your own behaviour bear fruit, you will find that your relationship with your children replaces the old hierarchy of threats and punishment. As restorative conversations coach new behaviours, children learn how to regulate themselves better. Everything becomes more rational, less emotional and much, much more positive.

When you get it right – when you avert morning Armageddon because you don't shout; when you notice gently and choose the right words – there is a small but tangible reward: that little feeling of achievement, bordering on smugness.

That glowing feeling is addictive and it doesn't diminish as things improve. As you get better at being calmer by default, it becomes easier to see your way through tricky moments. Being less hasty to react gives you time to think, time to plan, time to breathe. Enjoy that feeling. Remember how much better it is than the aftermath of shouting. Just be careful not to look too smug in public.

Change does take time, persistence and daily grind. But you can make a big step forward. Starting immediately.

The prize is not just better behaviour. The prize is your relationship with your child. Preserved and enhanced, even in the difficult moments. A relationship without shame or fear or the anxiety of inconsistency.

That prize is worth everything. So start today. Make a plan. Change some lives. Change everything.

ABOUT THE AUTHOR

After countless attempts to sabotage his own education, Paul Dix miraculously went on to train at Homerton College, Cambridge, before going on to work as a teacher at some of Britain's most challenging urban schools.

Over the next three decades, Paul would develop a unique approach to behaviour change – one rooted in the calm consistency of the adults. After outlining his method in the bestselling *When the Adults Change, Everything Changes*, it became a word-of-mouth phenomenon among teachers and has now been drawn upon in over 150,000 classrooms worldwide.

When, in 2002, Paul became a dad, he began to wonder whether his behaviour change method might just work for parents too. Now, for the first time, Paul introduces his findings to the most important audience of all: parents.